Digital Literacy

Mandy Reininger
Darrel Karbginsky

Digital Literacy
ISBN: 978-1-943536-31-3
Edition 1.0 Fall 2017

Chemeketa Press

Chemeketa Press is a nonprofit publishing endeavor at Chemeketa Community College. Working together with faculty, staff, and students, we develop and publish affordable and effective alternatives to commercial textbooks. All proceeds from the sale of this book will be used to develop new textbooks. To learn more, visit chemeketapress.org.

Publisher: Tim Rogers
Managing Editor: Steve Richardson
Production Editor: Brian Mosher
Editorial Assistant: Travis Willmore
Design Editor: Ronald Cox IV
Cover Design: Emily Evans
Interior Design and Layout: Michael Ovens, Matthew Sanchez, Shaun Jaquez
Image Generation: Cierra Maher, Kristi Etzel, Emily Evans, Faith Martinmaas, Candace Johnson, Michael Ovens, Keyiah McClain

Acknowledgments

Text and image acknowledgments appear on pages 133 to 148 and constitute an extension of this copyright page.

Additional contributions to the design and publication of this textbook came from students in the Visual Communications program at Chemeketa Community College.

Printed in the United States of America.

Contents

Chapter 1
Introduction to Computers

1. Introduction

One way you know that something is everywhere is when you stop noticing it. Computers are now one of those things. So many of the things we take for granted rely on computers to function. The fact that your car stereo can link with your smartphone is because of a computer. You can also use your phone to pay your electric bill. Just imagine how many mechanical and electrical processes have to be performed by computers to record the amount of electricity you use, send you a bill, and receive payment from your phone. From laptops to tablets and smartphones, mobile computing has made computer use something that happens every day, throughout the entire day.

At school, you see computing power at work when you watch a PowerPoint presentation or YouTube video in class. You see it again when you go to the library and look up information on academic databases. All throughout your day on campus, lights and climate control are at work and doors are remaining unlocked at the right times thanks to a computer system that oversees these systems.

At work, whether that's at an office or a restaurant or a store, you can be sure that there's at least one computer on the premises for processing financial transactions. And there are probably many more than that to help with security, accounting, ordering, and more.

In your free time, it's likely that a smartphone follows you wherever you go. You'll use it for much more than phone calls. You'll text with friends, look for places on maps, and stay connected to social media. The car you drive or the bus you ride has a computer performing engine-management duties. In this century, it takes work to *not* interact, directly or indirectly, with some form of computer power on a daily basis.

Things haven't been this way for very long. Just fifty years ago, if you used a computer, it was a big deal. The computer wouldn't have fit in your pocket or backpack, either. It took up an entire room, and was probably kept locked in a government building or a fancy executive office. Today, though, computers are much smaller and not just used for work. We use them to play games, to watch TV, to call our friends, to drive our cars while we call our friends. You can hardly look *anywhere* without seeing a computer — even refrigerators and toasters use them. They're involved in nearly every aspect of modern life.

Figure 1.

Figure 2. A Japanese ATM.

Figure 3. Most modern stereos are computers.

Figure 4. Smartphones are minicomputers.

Figure 5. Calculators are computers.

Because computers are all around you, it's important to know how to use them. When you need to write a paper, for example, knowing how to use a word processor will help you write and edit that paper more effectively. Word-processing programs like Microsoft Word also offer tools like spelling and grammar checkers, word and character counters, and pre-programmed document design styles. These all save you time and help you create a better paper.

It's also important to learn how computers work because people who lack this knowledge are at a disadvantage in the workplace and in daily life. As technology advances, the number of people who need to use computers is increasing. Computers have changed the way we work, but they've also changed the way we interact and the way we play — and some believe they've even changed the way we think about ourselves and our place in the world. If you're not comfortable with computers, you won't be comfortable at work or with the world around you.

This textbook as a whole is a guide to understanding and using computers. It gives you information to make you more comfortable using computers at an introductory level — and in some ways beyond a typical computer user's comfort level. It covers the basics of computer literacy, but it also explores the power of software, the vastness of networks, recent advancements in communication technology, and the importance of computer security in the changing world of privacy and surveillance.

We begin this chapter with what a computer is, what it can do, and where it came from.

What Is a Computer?

A computer is an automatic, electronic data-processing machine that takes in facts and figures called data, organizes or processes these data in some useful way, and then displays — or outputs — the results for you to see as information. The computer's original function was calculation (Figure 5). It made complex calculations more efficient by relieving people from spending many hours to manually complete the work. Today, a computer can still help with calculations, but it also facilitates communication and provides entertainment.

Figure 6. The four categories of functions on a laptop.

Figure 7. Standard Keyboard.

Figure 8. A computer mouse.

A computer's functions fit into four categories: receiving input, producing output, harnessing processing power, and managing storage (Figure 6).

Input refers to a computer's ability to receive instructions from user-controlled devices, like a keyboard, a mouse, a touch-screen monitor, or a gaming controller (Figure 7) to (Figure 9). You can think of input as the source of information being sent to the computer by the user. When you type on your keyboard or move your mouse, the computer receives that information as input and displays the results of your actions to you as output.

Figure 9. A gaming controller with keyboard attachment.

Output refers to the components a computer uses that send back information to the user based on the input received. The computer sends that information back on output devices like a monitor, printer, and speakers (Figure 10) to (Figure 12). Think of output as the result of the information you sent via input. But before it can become output, that information must be processed by the computer. We will explain the purpose of a wide variety of input and output devices in Chapter 2: "Basic Input and Output Components."

Processing is the computer's main job. Processing is when the computer creates and solves calculations based on commands from the input devices and programs being used by the computer. Processing happens in the central processing unit, or CPU.

Figure 10. Dual computer monitor setup.

The arithmetic logic unit (ALU), one component of the CPU, is the part of a computer that performs all arithmetic computations, such as addition and multiplication, and all comparison operations (Figure 13). Another component is the control unit (CU), which extracts instructions from memory (memory being the areas of the computer's hardware that store data where they can be used immediately) and decodes and executes these instructions, calling on the ALU when necessary.

Figure 11. Home or office printer.

Figure 12. USB speakers.

Figure 13. Computer CPU and chip.

Figure 14. A hard disk drive.

Figure 15. Compact discs.

Figure 16. USB flash drive.

The CPU is connected to the computer's **motherboard**, the hub where all other parts of the computer are connected to one another. All of a computer's components connect to the motherboard in one of two ways. One option is that they are connected directly by miniature pin connections inside the computer chassis — the physical case that contains most of the main components of the computer. The other option is that the components like keyboards, mice, speakers, and monitors are connected externally through USB ports, audio jacks, and Bluetooth connections. Either way, all the computer components are connected to the motherboard for processing.

Storage is the system that a computer uses to manage all the data that the computer processes into information. Storage comes in two forms — short-term memory and long-term memory. Short-term memory, also known as volatile memory because it requires a constant current from the power supply to keep it alive, is random-access memory (RAM) that allows different items of data to be accessed at roughly the same time, regardless of where they are stored. Long-term memory, also known as persistent memory, is stored on a hard disk drive (HDD), which can be internal or external, a compact disk drive (CDD) such as a CD or DVD, or a USB flash drive (Figure 14) to (Figure 16). Programs on a computer can compute faster by immediately storing and retrieving data and information in the RAM storage in small chunks, but if users need to save data or information for later use, they can do so on an HDD, a CDD, or a flash drive.

Data vs. Information

Data, which is plural for "datum," are the raw, unorganized facts that are put into a computer. This doesn't mean that only input devices deliver data. Programs and operating systems also transfer data whenever they are in use. Massive amounts of data are inputted into a computer whenever it is completing any kind of process. The computer then calculates the data. It processes, organizes, and structures the data within a given context in order to provide meaningful and useful calculation of data. This meaningful and useful output is called information (Figure 17). It informs the user.

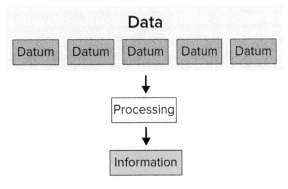

Figure 17. Datums to data.

An example of data is a list of rainfall amounts for every day in a year. Each rainfall amount is a datum. Taken together, you have 365 data. But these data by themselves don't inform you. They are just a list of numbers. A computer, however, can process these numbers for you and provide you with meaningful calculations such as the total amount of rain for the year or the average daily rainfall or how much rain fell in February. The processed data is information. It informs you.

Another example is a list of all the first names in Social Security applications in Oregon for 2015. Each name is a datum. Taken by itself, you have another long list of data:

Liam	Arlo	JoJo
Henry	Emma	Penelope
Ava	Sebastian	Liam
Emma	Olivia	Ella
William	Liam	Ava
Elijah	Emma	Liam
...	...	...

If you input these data into a computer, however, the computer can add up how many times each name appears, sort the names from most used to least used, and give you the information:

The most popular male name is Liam (222).

The most popular female name is Emma (234).

These processed data are now useful, especially if you're looking for a popular name for your cat in 2015. The computer has given you information.

Data are inputted into a computer as a set of numbers, letters, or characters. Those symbols are then translated into binary code, which records data using a series of zeros and ones. One piece of binary information is called a bit. It can be either a zero or a one. Eight bits of information make a byte. As computing has become more complex and requires more and more binary digits to transmit the necessary code, prefixes to "bit" and "byte" have started piling up in order to quantify the amount of binary data at work. "Kilo" means one thousand (as in "kilobits" or "kilobytes"), "mega" means one million, "giga" means one billion, and "tera" means one trillion. Petabytes, exabytes, zettabytes and yottabytes are further exponential increases in magnitude of data.

Computer programs and languages then process this raw binary information and conduct calculations. The results are then translated from binary code into the words and numbers and often the sentences that inform you. Those useful, processed data have become information.

2. A Brief History of Computing

The abacus, the slide rule, and the electronic calculator are all historical evidence of humans' innate drive to find new ways to solve problems, be more productive, work with numbers faster, and improve data storage. The creation of more and more complex tools to more efficiently harness the power of our minds has never stopped, or even slowed down, in recorded history.

The Pursuit of Computation

Figure 18. Pascal's Numverical Wheel, or Pascaline.

The first computers were mechanical devices that performed calculations and were sometimes prone to errors.

In 1642, Blaise Pascal built a numerical wheel-adding machine to help his father's work as a tax collector. It was a heavy burden to add numbers by hand, and Pascal saw his machine as a chance to relieve that burden. He built twenty of these machines, which are called the Pascaline (Figure 18).

Figure 19. Leibniz's calculator.

A few years later, in 1673, Gottfried Wilhelm von Leibniz, a German mathematician, built a calculating device that could add, subtract, multiply, and divide (Figure 19). It provided more functions than Pascal's machine and allowed users to solve more types of problems. Both Pascal's and Leibniz's machines were flawed, however, and not dependable.

Another important innovation came from Joseph Jacquard, a French weaver, who designed a punch card loom in 1805 (Figure 20). A chain of punch cards in a certain order provided instructions for the loom's weaving pattern. The pattern could be changed by using different cards in different orders. This discovery eventually led to storing computer instructions on cards like Jacquard's.

Charles Xavier Thomas, another Frenchman, developed a new mechanical computer. He called it the "four-function machine," and it was more reliable than Pascal's or Leibniz's machines. By 1820, technology and material quality had improved after lessons

Figure 20. Jacquard's loom.

were learned from those other machines' flaws (Figure 21).

One of the largest contributions to computation came with the "Difference Engine" invented by Charles Babbage and Ada Lovelace in 1842. This was an automatic logarithm tabulator and printer (Figure 22). It had a memory unit, automatic printout, sequential program control in which one operation was performed at a time, and punch-card input. The punch card idea was borrowed from Jacquard's loom. The Difference Engine was a milestone for women in computer history because Lovelace suggested that a binary system of numbers be used, which set the standard that is still used today.

However, the Difference Engine never really worked. The machining technology needed to create proper gears and shafts was not good enough or precise enough for the accuracy that the machine required. Even so, its design helped pave the way for future computers. The IBM Corporation was later able to build a working model of the Difference Engine using modernized parts.

Early Innovations

In 1936, the pioneer computer theorist Alan Turing invented what he called the "a-machine," which was short for "automatic machine." This was a more of a formal model for testing algorithms than a physical machine, although physical examples have been built. The machine operated on an infinite strip of memory tape divided into individual sections. The machine read each of these sections, or cells, and performed one of a limited number of functions based on what kind of data were in each cell. The Turing machine was enormously influential on the direction of theoretical computer science.

Figure 21. Charles Thomas' four-function machine.

Figure 22. Babbage and Lovelace's Difference Engine.

Figure 23. Vacuum tubes or valves.

After World War II, the science of building physical computers also experienced radical change. The vacuum tube, also known as a valve because it controls the flow of electrons like a faucet controls water flow, was originally developed to amplify and demodulate — or "detect" — radio signals. Once the war ended, computers were built using these tubes.

The sheer number of logic functions computers could do meant that very large numbers of tubes were needed (Figure 23). A considerable amount of heat was produced when the tubes operated. This came both from the filament, which was like the filament in a light bulb, and from the stream of electrons bombarding the plate. Plates attract electrons but do not emit any of their own. Damage from excess heat caused tubes to be unreliable in

Figure 24. Replica of the first transistor.

Figure 25. Integrated circuit from an EPROM memory microship.

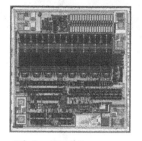

Figure 26. A microchip.

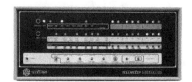

Figure 27. Altair.

Figure 28. Radio Shack's TRS-80.

most operations, which limited the effectiveness of these early computers.

A replacement for vacuum tubes soon developed. **Transistors** bypassed the limitations of vacuum tubes and began the process of reducing the size of computers (Figure 24). A transistor is a solid-state amplifier that serves as a kind of logic gate. Most transistors used in computer processors are either fully on or fully off. These types of transistors do not need to heat a filament, nor must they open or close physical contacts to cause a change in electron flow.

Transistors are the main component in an **integrated circuit** (IC). The earliest ICs contained only a few transistors, but in less than twenty years, ICs with over 100,000 transistors were created. The size of transistors limited the number that could be placed on early ICs, but as transistors shrank, the number that could be contained on an IC increased (Figure 25).

Today, several billion transistors can fit on an integrated circuit the size of a human fingernail. The comparably vast number of transistors available on these circuits led to the name **microchip** to describe the circuits. Microchips are also integrated circuits, but because microchips' capabilities are so greatly improved, they now go by this name to distinguish them from the early ICs (Figure 26).

Rise of the Microcomputer

Introduced in 1975, the **Altair** is considered the first home computer. Its only input was a series of front-panel switches (Figure 27). However, it had a motherboard with a **bus** — a communication pathway that transfers data within a computer or between several computers — that allowed other companies to provide keyboards, tape readers, and other devices to access the registers, locations easily accessible to the CPU. A group of Harvard students — Steve Ballmer, Paul Allen, and Bill Gates — left school to focus on code development for the Altair and created Microsoft not long after.

In 1977, Radio Shack released its own microcomputer, the **TRS-80**, with the help of retailer Tandy Corporation (Figure 28). The single-color screen, cassette tape drive, and unusual keyboard didn't keep the TRS-80 from being the best-selling PC through 1982. Released in 1977 to compete with the TRS-80, the **Apple II** stayed a major staple in the PC market throughout the 1980s with several series upgrades (Figure 29). It was a major advancement over the Apple I, a bare circuit board machine intended mostly for electronics hobbyists. The Apple II's best feature was the ability to display color through its use of then-modern television output.

The **IBM PC** of 1981 was the product of a company that had been around since 1911, acting as a front-runner in the development of mainframes and early computers for business (Figure 30). The IBM PC was a personal computer built around the Intel 8088 microprocessor. This is important because the PC became standardized, and today the majority of personal computers are IBM-compatible.

Figure 29. Apple II.

The 1982 **Commodore 64**, which sold 22 million units, was the most significant of Commodore's PC models (Figure 31). The Commodore 64 was sold in retail stores instead of just electronics or computer stores, opening a wider world of middle-class households to the new technology. The availability of games for the Commodore 64 expanded the uses of computers to include entertainment.

Figure 30. Commodore 64.

Best known for its video game consoles, **Atari** began with two 8-bit computers, the 400 and 800 PC, in 1979. Between 1979 and 1984, Atari released several PC models based on their 8-bit line, but the 16/32-bit system released in 1985, the Atari ST, was a notable development in the history of microcomputers (Figure 32). It led to other popular game consoles from Atari.

3. Types of Computers

Figure 31. One of Atari's PC models.

Of the many types of computers, you will recognize quite a few as computers you already use. Others have more specialized purposes and require a surprising amount of processing power. The most prominent computer types for the average individual user are smartphones, tablets, laptops, and desktops. For people and companies in need of more power than one personal computer can provide, there are servers, mainframes and supercomputers. Understanding a computer's design tells us a lot about how it's used.

Figure 32. IBM PC.

Gaming Consoles

Digital gaming has come a long way since the days of Atari. The main difference between a video game console and a personal computer is the user interface. Like a personal computer, a game console contains computing hardware and some form of visual display. However, the way that users interact with a gaming console's computer is a controller or joystick containing multiple buttons and functions, rather than a keyboard and mouse.

A gaming console, as the name implies, is also designed primarily for playing computer games, and it is not generally set up for things like word processing or other functions typically done at work or school on a desktop or laptop computer. Some of the most popular gaming console systems include various derivations of the Sony PlayStation, Microsoft XBOX, and Nintendo Wii, handheld DS and Switch.

Smartphones and Smartwatches

A smartphone is a mobile device that acts as a combined telephone and personal digital assistant (PDA). PDA refers to any mobile device that manages information digitally. Like tablets, smartphones generally have a touch screen, and like laptops, PDAs, and most tablets, smartphones have a battery so that you can use them without constantly plugging them into a wall outlet for power. Smartphones use liquid-crystal display (LCD) screens because LCDs are thinner and require less energy than more traditional screen types (Figure 33).

Figure 33. Android smartphones.

Figure 34. Apple smartphones.

Smartphones generally use one of five common operating systems: Android, iOS, Blackberry OS, Symbian OS or Windows. An operating system is the governing software that manages the computer's data and converts those data into information. These operating systems manage the applications — or apps — on the smartphone. Apps are the programs that smartphones users rely on to make phone calls, send text messages, browse the Internet, or perform any of the other operations of smartphones in today's technology-heavy world. Smartphones are such a key part of that world because they're even more portable than a tablet or laptop. A smartphone typically fits in a purse or pocket, and can be taken most anywhere (Figure 34).

Smart devices that the user can wear are now at the forefront of computing technology. A smartwatch does a great deal more than simply tell a user what time it is — although smartwatches do tell time with the accuracy of an atomic clock. Beyond timekeeping, early smartwatch versions were capable only of performing simple functions like calculations, translating, and simple gameplay.

However, the newest models can do most anything a full-blown computer can do. They can function as a cell phone, GPS, memory card, rechargeable battery, altimeter, barometer, and more. Some can be used as portable music players and play digital music files or FM radio to a wireless headset. Smartwatches are now like personal computers that can be worn on your wrist.

Tablets

Tablet PCs are typically smaller than laptops and have a special screen that can accept touch input from a user's fingers or a stylus — a pen-shaped device that sends commands to a computer by touching the screen. No mouse or external keyboard is required, but a keyboard is usually optional. Common interfaces include Amazon's Kindle, Google's Android, Microsoft's Windows, and Apple's iOS.

Figure 35. A tablet computer.

Tablets are usually more powerful than smartphones but are still quite mobile. They are typically the size of a magazine or small book and can be loaded with various apps that will perform many of the functions of smartphones or laptops. Reader apps, for example, allow a tablet to be used for reading stored text information (Figure 36). Tablets are generally used for browsing the Internet, sending messages, reading books, streaming videos, or playing games.

Laptops

A laptop is a portable computer that provides many benefits to users who need to work from multiple physical locations. Users who need a laptop for art and design, for gaming, or for basic web browsing will each benefit from a different type of laptop (Figure 35).

Some computer manufacturers market **design laptops** to an "artist user," someone who needs a laptop able to handle running programs that aid artistic purposes like photo editing, graphic design, game design, or audio and video editing. Packing the same

Figure 36. Laptop computers are good for users who need to be mobile.

amount of power into the smaller form of a laptop makes a comparably powerful laptop more expensive than its desktop counterpart. However, artists or designers might prefer a mobile computer so they can work from a variety of locations, such as on location for filming or at a sponsoring studio space with other artists.

A **gaming laptop** is used primarily for playing video games and typically needs a fast, powerful graphics-processing unit (GPU) that is separate from the main CPU. Users may also choose to increase available RAM and store game files on faster long-term storage options like a solid-state drive to decrease loading times for the game's content. Mobile laptop gaming computers are sometimes less powerful than their desktop counterparts, but the ability to travel and play is appealing to many people, especially those who can find reliable Internet access for online games outside their home.

Average laptop users need a **basic laptop** that can run their Internet browser and any productivity software they like. While not necessarily required, increased RAM is a wise choice for most users because the average user tends to run multiple applications at once. Multitasking is important in current computer use, and RAM size impacts users' ability to work on their word processors, check their email, and stream music or video all at the same time.

Desktops

Desktop PCs are computers that you don't move around. They generally are a box with a separate monitor connected, but some all-in-one computers have all the computer hardware built behind the monitor. While desktops have less mobility, their size allows greater storage and processing power. Desktop designs vary widely depending on whether they are used for basic home use, for gaming, or for more power-intensive engineering and design programs. While the uses for desktops include all of the above laptop uses, desktops are also available in the following categories: a workstation, a gaming desktop, a NUC, and a Raspberry Pi.

A "power user" is someone who needs to run graphics-intensive programs like computer-drafting software for engineers and builders. Power users need computers with higher levels of power to display those programs. These computers, called **workstations**, are expensive compared to other computer types, in many cases costing several thousand dollars. Workstations are large, extremely powerful computers for intensive visual or mathematical operations. They are used by designers, engineers, and manufacturers to complete projects that include making physical models from data. Similarly, the computers that store and manage banking information must be very powerful to run numerous mathematical operations simultaneously (Figure 37).

Figure 37. Desktop computers are powerful but stationary.

Like a gaming laptop, a **gaming desktop** needs to have a separate graphics processor, additional memory, and a fast storage drive like a solid-state drive for fast loading times. Some gaming computers use specialized input devices, like a gaming mouse or gaming keyboard, that feature specialized functions to assist players of specific games.

Figure 38. A NUC next to a roll of 35mm film for scale.

The **Next Unit of Computing** (NUC) is a small, specialized PC for targeted purposes (Figure 38). An average user's purposes could likely be met with a NUC, but these devices' small size makes them especially useful for home theater PCs (HTPCs) that mostly stream video, or for offices with crowded desk space. Some technicians who specialize in troubleshooting larger electronic devices use NUCs because of their portability and their quick setup and use.

While a NUC desktop could probably meet the needs of the average desktop user, the small form adds to their cost and is not the most common type for average users at this point. The average desktop contains a low-level processor, but may have increased memory because of the average user's desire to multitask, requiring extra memory while multiple applications are in use at once.

Since 2012, the **Raspberry Pi** — or Pi, as it is often called — has been used to promote teaching computer science in schools and developing countries. The attraction is its low cost. The price for a Pi ranges from $10 for the Raspberry Pi Zero W to $35 for the Raspberry Pi 3 (Figure 39) and (Figure 40). These come with built-in WiFi and Bluetooth capability. You still need an HDMI monitor, a keyboard, and a mouse, but with some savvy shopping you can find these items new for under $80 total. The Pi uses the Raspbian operating system — a Debian-based Linux operating system developed by the Raspberry Pi Foundation — and can also use third-party operating systems such as Ubuntu, Windows 10 IOT Core, and RISC OS. The Raspbian and Ubuntu operating systems come complete with multimedia, game, educational, office, communication, internet, networking, and tools utilities software. In addition, Raspbian comes with tools for programming in Python, Java, and Scratch.

Figure 39. Raspberry Pi Zero W shown with a US quarter for size comparison.

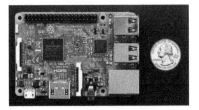

Figure 40. Raspberry Pi 3 shown with a US quarter for size comparison.

Servers

A server is a computer program or device that provides functions — services — for other programs or devices, which are called "clients." This relationship is known as the client–server model. Services can include sharing data, information, or resources among multiple clients or performing computation for a client. A single server can serve multiple clients, and a single client can use multiple servers. A client may access a server on the same device, or may connect over a network to a server on a different device. There are several types of servers, but none are mobile (Figure 41).

Figure 41. Rows of computer servers.

Different kinds of computer servers are like the parts of a restaurant. A network server is like a restaurant's physical building. You have to be there to use the restaurant. A web server is like the human servers working in the restaurant. You tell them what you want, and they bring it to you. If you've ordered in the right way, the service will probably be better and faster. Computer servers provide the information you want, but you have to ask the right way. File servers are like the walk-in refrigerator in the restaurant's kitchen that stores everything you could possibly want to order from the restaurant.

Figure 42. A typical server rack.

A **network server** is a central point for accessing applications and data. Other more specific types of servers can be attached to a network server for access by multiple users at once (Figure 42). For this reason, network servers are often used by system administrators for large organizations' networks that contain a high number of individual computers. The network server is typically a high-performance personal computer itself.

The primary function of a **web server** is to store, process, and deliver web pages to clients. The communication between client and server takes place using protocols — the rules a communication must follow in order to be sent and delivered correctly. The most common type of web server communication is a web page, which is delivered in a protocol called HTML. HTML documents may include images, style sheets, and scripts, in addition to the text content of a page. If you are surfing the web, you are accessing new web servers with every new page you visit. Any person or organization who hosts a website, then, is using a web server. For an especially high-traffic website like Facebook or Wikipedia, multiple web servers may be used for one site.

Web servers are not only used for serving the World Wide Web. They can also be found embedded in devices such as printers, webcams, and routers — networking devices that send data from computer to computer. They can serve a local network that isn't connected to the Internet and be part of a system for monitoring or administering the devices connected to it. This usually means that no additional software has to be installed on the client computer, since only a web browser is required. Web browsers are now included on most operating systems. This means that you as the typical home user probably make use of a web server, whether you know it or not.

File servers generally serve large groups of users accessing shared files and folders stored on the server (Figure 43). A file server is not intended to perform computational tasks and does not run programs on behalf of its clients, but is designed primarily to enable the storage and retrieval of data while the computers connected to it do the computation work. File servers are likely to be seen in settings like schools and offices because those are environments where a local area network (LAN), which is not connected to the World Wide Web, is used to connect multiple users.

Figure 43. A file server primarily acts as data storage.

Mainframes

Mainframe computers are used primarily by large organizations for critical applications. Mainframes process bulk data such as census, industry, and consumer statistics. They support business management software that can deal with many types of data simultaneously, and they process complex business and governmental transactions (Figure 44).

The term "mainframe" originally referred to the large, cabinet-like structures — the main frames — that housed the CPUs and main memory of early computers. Later, as computers became smaller, the term was used to distinguish large, high-end commercial machines from smaller and less powerful computers.

Mainframe computers operate like the network servers described in the previous section. Both are used for similar types of data processing, but they do so on vastly different scales. A mainframe typically has hundreds or even thousands of times more data storage than a network server being run on a desktop computer. Whether an organization puts the extra effort and expense into running an actual mainframe will depend on the size and frequency of the computing tasks that need to be performed.

Supercomputers

A supercomputer is a computer with computational capacity that is much higher than a general-purpose mainframe computer. Most large-scale computer system architectures were established in the 1960s, and they continued to evolve into today's supercomputers. Mainframes are used to process transactions, and supercomputers deal with complex mathematical equations.

The performance of a supercomputer is measured in floating-point operations per second (FLOPS) instead of million instructions per second (MIPS). As of 2015, there are supercomputers that can perform up to several quadrillions of FLOPS. That's essentially around 120,000 times faster than a normal but still powerful desktop computer (Figure 45).

Figure 44. Workers in an early mainframe.

Figure 45. IBM supercomputer.

Chapter 2

Basic Input and Output Components

It takes more than the right combination of ones and zeroes to make a computer useful. For the computer to process data smoothly, the actual physical parts of the computer must work in harmony, too. These physical components are called hardware. This chapter builds on the first chapter's discussion of input and output by explaining how hardware — disk drives, monitors, hard drives, mice, and so on — helps to input data into a computer, store those data, and output information within a single computer or among multiple computers.

1. Input Hardware

Before a computer can start to compute, it needs some data to work with, and that's why we start with input hardware. These are the devices that capture data and send those data into memory and storage hardware so that the computer's processor can make sense of it and output information.

Keyboard

A **keyboard** is an input device which is connected to a computer and is used to type instructions or other input into the computer (Figure 1). Typically, a keyboard has about 100 keys. Keyboards can be wired by being plugged into a USB or other connector to the motherboard, or wireless by connecting to the motherboard via Wi-Fi or Bluetooth signal technology (see "Wireless Devices" later in this chapter). Keyboards are available in many forms — desktop keyboards, tablet attachments, ergonomic keyboards for avoiding repetitive movement injuries, and gaming keyboards with backlit keys and software to initiate complex commands with just one button. Many keyboards have a function key (FN) for controlling hot keys such as email, audio and Internet browser. These keys can typically be customized to suit your needs, thus making the keyboard more functional. (Table 1) provides some common keyboard shortcuts.

Figure 1. A wireless Apple keyboard.

An **ergonomic keyboard** is designed to minimize muscle strain and related problems like carpal tunnel syndrome, typically by using a V-shape that allows the user's right and left hands to each be at a more natural angle to the keyboard. There are two main types of ergonomic keyboards. The split keyboard has two groups of keys, one on the right and one on the left. The contoured keyboard places keys into two sets of depressions in the surface of the keyboard rather than on a flat surface.

Function	Windows Shortcut	Mac Shortcut
Cut: Remove the selected item and copy it to the Clipboard	Ctrl-X	Command-X
Copy the selected item to the Clipboard.	Ctrl-C	Command-C
Paste the contents of the Clipboard into the current document.	Ctrl-V	Command-V
Undo the previous command.	Ctrl-Z	Command-Z
Select all items.	Ctrl-A	Command-A
New: Open a new document or window.	Ctrl-N	Command-N
Open the selected item, or open a dialog to select a file to open.	Ctrl-O	Command-O
Print the current document.	Ctrl-P	Command-P
Save the current document.	Ctrl-S	Command-S
Close the active window.	Alt-F4	Command-W

Table 1. Common keyboard shortcuts.

Mouse

A **mouse** is a user interface device that can enable different kinds of control than a keyboard can, particularly with operating systems and software that allow users to interact with graphical icons and indicators rather than just text (Figure 2).

A computer mouse can be used to give four basic instructions to your computer: left-click, double-click, right-click, and drag. Each of these instructions indicates using a combination of buttons on the device and moving the mouse to the desired location in the interface (Table 2). As with keyboards, many pointing devices have more than just the basic functions. The extra buttons can be configured to a user's needs, increasing the functionality of the mouse.

An **optical mouse** uses a light source, typically an LED, and a light detector, such as an array of photodiodes, to detect movement relative to a surface. It is an alternative to the mechanical mouse, which uses moving parts to sense motion.

Figure 2. A variety of computer mice.

Another kind of motion control device that performs the same job as a mouse is a **touchpad**, or trackpad. This is a pointing device featuring a tactile sensor, a specialized surface that can translate the motion and position of a user's fingers to a relative position on the operating

Left-Click	Used primarily to select or activate the icons in the interface.
Right-Click	Typically opens optional actions within an icon or field.
Double-Click	Two left-clicks in rapid succession. Typically executes the primary function of the icon, whether opening a file, opening a folder, or starting a program.
Drag	Hold down a left- or right-click and move the mouse. This selects and "grabs" the icon you're working with, allowing you to move it to other locations. Left-click drag will move an icon around your interface area, while right-click drag will move the icon and offer a list of options on release of the click, such as copy, move, or create a shortcut link between the two locations.

Table 2. Mouse instructions.

system that is outputted to the screen. Touchpads are a common feature of laptop computers, and are also used as a substitute for a mouse when desk space is scarce (Figure 3).

A **trackball mouse** is a derivative of the mouse concept in which the base of the device stays in one place and a ball on top of the base is manipulated by the user's fingers to move the mouse icon displayed on the computer's monitor. A trackball can be more versatile than a traditional mouse because there is no limit to its range of movement. It does not have to be picked up off the desk and set down again to keep moving.

Figure 3. Laptops are commonly equipped with a trackpad.

Digital Camera

Digital cameras store images digitally rather than recording them on film. Once a digital picture has been captured, it can be downloaded to a computer system, manipulated with a graphics program, and printed. Unlike film photographs, which have an almost infinite resolution, digital photos are limited by the amount of memory in the camera, the optical resolution of the digitizing mechanism, and ultimately by the resolution of the final output device. Typical digital cameras are either point-and-shoot or DSLR.

Figure 4. A point-and-shoot camera.

Point-and-shoot cameras are generally designed to be compact, stylish, and easy to use (Figure 4). They tend to have very basic user control with predefined capture modes, and they often don't allow for much manual adjustment. Typically, these cameras have more megapixels, resulting in high resolutions, but less overall image quality than DSLR cameras.

Figure 5. One model of DSLR camera.

Figure 6. A computer webcam.

Digital single lens reflex (DSLR) cameras are customizable and intended for use by professional photographers (Figure 5). These cameras have a through-the-lens rather than an over-the-lens viewfinder, resulting in photos that accurately show what the photographer sees when looking through the viewfinder. DSLRs are available with interchangeable lenses and contain image sensors that are much larger and better constructed than those in point-and-shoot cameras. The result is higher image quality.

A **webcam** is a video and audio capture device that connects to a computer, usually via a USB port (Figure 6). A webcam transmits what it captures in its lens to the computer as an image. Webcams are commonly used to take pictures quickly or to stream video chat between users.

When purchasing a digital camera, many users focus on its size, but you should also assess technical specifications like megapixels for still photos and frames per second for video. A megapixel represents one million independent points — or pixels — in an image, each of which incorporates color, brightness, hue, and luminosity. The more pixels used to represent an image, the sharper and more distinct that image will be when printed. The more pixels used, the larger the printed image can be without becoming pixelated.

Frames per second means the number of still frames that a device can capture to simulate movement during video playback. Older film cameras were limited to 24 frames per second, causing the well-known "flicker" of old film technology. A modern film projection displays forty-eight frames per second, and the human eye can barely see the flicker. At sixty or more frames per second, no flicker is visible to the human eye. Today's computer hardware can go well beyond that to display upwards of 120 frames per second, depending on resolution and graphical demands. A digital camera that captures 48 frames per second will nearly always be enough for most purposes, but the frame speeds needed for high-resolution image capture may be harder to reach.

The Intel RealSense 3D camera is included with many higher end computers, both desktop and laptop models, and provides the ability to achieve depth perception, 3D imaging, interior mapping and feature tracking such as hand and eye movements. If a Windows 10 Professional computer is equipped with an Intel RealSense camera, you can use the Windows Hello feature to log onto your computer using 3D face recognition.

Scanner

A **scanner** is a device that optically scans images, printed text, handwriting, or an object, and converts the image to a digital image. **Flatbed scanners** are some of the most commonly used scanners because they have both home and office functions (Figure 7). They scan documents with a light source, a lens, and a light sensor that moves back and forth under the document to capture the image. **Document scanners** work like flatbed scanners, but the scanning light and sensor do not move. The document moves through the scanner and across the light instead of the light moving across the document. This type of scanner is useful for single sheets of paper, not for books or other bound material.

Figure 7. A flatbed scanner.

A **barcode scanner** can read printed barcodes and input those codes numerically into a computer (Figure 8). Like a flatbed scanner, it consists of a light source, a lens, and a light sensor translating optical information into electrical information. Barcode scanners are now almost universally connected to cash registers in retail stores, but they can also be used as handheld devices connected to desktop computers.

Figure 8. A barcode scanner.

Radio-frequency identification (RFID) uses electromagnetic fields to automatically identify and track tags attached to objects. The tags contain an integrated circuit and an antenna, which transmits its electronically stored information when it receives the radio signal from a nearby RFID reader. Passive, unpowered tags use energy from the RFID reader's radio waves (Figure 9). Many industrial applications use RFID. RFID tags attached to a car during production can be scanned later to track its progress through the assembly line. RFID-tagged pharmaceuticals can be tracked through warehouses and storage areas. Implanting RFID microchips in livestock and pets allows positive identification of animals.

Figure 9. A radio-frequency identification chip.

Figure 10. A laptop docked on a docking station.

Other Input Devices

A **docking station** is a device that features plug-and-play technology to detect and connect other devices like digital cameras or tablets. The docking station connects easily to a computer — often a laptop — for transferring files, charging the device's battery, and operating the device. Many stations are designed to cradle a connected laptop and charge its battery quickly and easily (Figure 10).

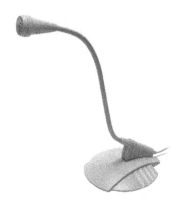

Figure 11. A "gooseneck" computer microphone.

Figure 12. A graphics tablet.

Figure 13. Using a tablet by hand.

Figure 14. Tablets can be used with fingers or styluses.

A **microphone** is a sensor that converts acoustic sound to an electrical signal. Many types and sizes of microphones are available to consumers, from headset microphones connected to headphone speakers to larger, free-standing microphones for more precise, clear audio capture (Figure 11).

A **graphics tablet**, also known as a pen tablet or digitizing tablet, is a pen-based input device. Once the tablet is connected to a computer via a USB port, a user can sketch or write anything on the tablet surface, and the computer will automatically display the image or writing on the computer's display (Figure 12). The tablet can also deliver commands to the computer like a mouse would. Professional artists or designers who work with pen and paper — such as cartoon animators, photo editors, and graphic artists — are the typical users of graphics tablets because a graphics tablet's main purpose is to add pen-like input to a computer.

Touchscreens and **touchpads** are devices that a user can interact with simply by touching the screen with fingers or a stylus to control the device's input (Figure 13). With touchscreens and touchpads, the typical input actions of a computer mouse are mimicked by finger gestures for scrolling up and down, shifting from side to side, and clicking. Touchpads are usually rectangular and are becoming very common in standalone devices. A **stylus** is a type of digital, electronic, or tablet pen that can be used with touchscreen devices to turn them into small graphics tablets. With very small screens, a stylus also allows more precise input than is possible with a finger (Figure 14).

A **remote control** is an electronic device that's used to operate another device from a short distance. This includes remote controls on television sets, movie players, and other home appliances. Remote controls for these devices are generally small, wireless, handheld objects with an array of buttons for adjusting various settings. For some devices, the remote control contains all the function controls of the main device, while the controlled device itself has only a handful of essential primary controls (Figure 15). Typical remote controls send digitally-coded pulses of infrared radiation to control functions such as power, volume, tuning, temperature, fan speed, and other features. This infrared light is invisible to the human eye, but sensors on the receiving device see the diode as if it were producing visible purple light.

Game controllers, or gamepads, capture users' input with buttons and one or more thumb sticks that act like joysticks (Figure 16). A joystick is a specific kind of gamepad, modeled after flight controllers in airplanes, that attempts to capture movement in two directions. There are many different types of game controllers, and as different gaming systems have evolved, these controllers have become more distinct from one another.

A **biometric device** is a security identification and authentication device. Automated measurements verify or recognize a person's identity based on a physiological or behavioral characteristic. These devices are capable of analyzing things like fingerprints, facial images, iris prints, and voices (Figure 17).

Figure 15. Remote controls are used to operate electronics from a distance.

Adaptive computer devices, also called assistive technology, consist of any device that is used to help individuals with disabilities maintain, increase, or improve their use of electronics. Common computer-related assistive technology products include screen magnifiers and large-key keyboards, as well as alternative input devices such as touchscreen displays, oversized trackballs and joysticks, speech recognition programs, and text readers.

There are also an increasing number of non-assistive applications for adaptive devices, including eye trackers. **Eye trackers** measure eye positions and eye movement by taking a reading of the motion of the eye relative to the head. They can then tell a computer what the user wants to do simply by determining where the user is looking on the screen. Another non-assistive adaptive device is a **speech-recognition** system. Speech recognition technology enables a computer to recognize spoken text and translate it into written language. Popular consumer versions include Siri and Cortana. Voice identification for security purposes works on similar principles. It determines who is speaking to the computer by measuring the qualities of a person's voice.

Figure 16. A variety of gaming controllers.

Figure 17. A fingerprint scanner is a type of biometric security device.

2. Storage Hardware

Storage hardware captures input data for the computer to process and then stores information for later output. With optical drives, data stored on existing discs can be inputted into the computer with a laser reader and new information can be stored on new discs. With hard drives and flash memory, the data and information are more fluid. They can be stored and erased and replaced by other data and information.

Optical Disc Drives

An optical disc drive is a storage device that allows the user to input and work with data that have been stored on removable media in a disc form. An optical laser device inside the drive reads the disc and inputs it into the computer for processing. There are several different types of optical drives, but each type can read multiple kinds of media (Figure 18).

A **compact disc** (CD) is a digital optical disc format for storing data. CDs have been a popular choice for storing music and other audio data for many years, but they are now much less popular for computer uses because other types of optical discs have much larger storage capacity than a CD. The maximum storage size of the twelve-centimeter disc is 700 MB.

Figure 18. A compact disc drive.

A CD-ROM disc is a pre-pressed optical disc that contains data. The name is an acronym for Compact Disc Read-Only Memory. Computers can read CD-ROMs, but they can't write to CD-ROMs because these discs are not writable or erasable. A CD-R (Compact Disc-Recordable) disc is another digital optical disc storage format that can be written only once and after that can only be read. The CD-RW (Compact Disc-ReWritable) can be written, read, erased, and written again.

DVD-ROM is a digital optical disc storage format that can store any kind of digital data. It is widely used for software and other computer files, and it's used to record movies and other video programs that can be viewed with DVD software or in DVD players. Even though DVDs are the same size as CDs, they can store much more data. A single-sided, single-layer DVD can store 4.7 GB of data, and a double-sided, single-layer DVD can store 9.4 GB.

DVD-ROM discs can only be read by a computer or DVD player. Recordable DVD discs (DVD-R and DVD+R) can be recorded once using a DVD recorder and then function as DVD-ROMs. Rewritable DVDs (DVD-RW, DVD+RW, and DVD-RAM) can be recorded and erased many times.

Blu-ray (BD, BRD) is another digital optical disc data storage format. It was designed to replace the DVD format with something capable of storing high-definition video resolution. Like DVDs, BDs store data in multiple layers, but because this is the most recent consumer technology, the amount of data is still growing as developers push the medium to its limits. Single-layer BDs can store 25 GB of data. Dual-layer BDs can store 50 GB of data, and as of early 2016, quad-layer BDs were becoming available with 100 GB of storage capacity for use with 4K-resolution film releases. The number of layers possible appears to be growing, too. Tech companies have successfully experimented with a six-layer BD that achieves 200 GB storage capacity by using six 33 GB layers.

BD-R (Blu-ray Disc Recordable) discs can be written to once and can then only be read. BD-RE (Blu-ray Disc Recordable Erasable) can be erased and re-recorded multiple times.

Figure 19. An internal hard drive.   **Figure 20.** An external hard drive.   **Figure 21.** Solid state drives contain no moving parts.

Hard Drives

A **hard disk drive** (HDD) — also called a hard disk, hard drive, or fixed disk — is a data-storage device for storing and retrieving digital information using one or more rigid spinning disks, known as platters, that are coated with magnetic material. The platters rotate at different speeds depending on the drive. Common speeds for mechanical drives are 5400, 7200, and 10,000 revolutions per minute. The platters are paired with magnetic heads arranged on a moving arm. These heads read and write data to the platter surfaces. The faster the rotation speed, the faster the disk can read and write data.

Data are accessed in a random-access manner, so individual blocks of data can be stored or retrieved in any order, not just sequentially. HDDs retain stored data even when they are powered off. HDDs are available as internal and external mechanical drives, but they are becoming increasingly outmoded as solid-state drive technology becomes more affordable for consumer users.

Internal hard drives are stored inside the computer chassis and are typically connected by SATA connecter cables for power and data transfer (Figure 19). **External hard drives** remain outside the computer case in a case of their own and are connected to the motherboard by a USB, Firewire, or e-SATA cable (see "Connecting Devices to a Computer" later in this chapter) for data transfer and a discrete power supply (Figure 20).

A **solid-state drive** (SSD) contains neither an actual disk nor a drive motor to spin a disk. In fact, SSDs have *no* moving parts. Instead, they use integrated circuit assemblies as their memory. SSD technology primarily uses electronic interfaces compatible with the traditional block input and output of hard disk drives, allowing for a simple replacement of those mechanical drives in most computers (Figure 21).

SSDs are much faster on average than mechanical drives, typically capable of data transfer more than three times the speed of a mechanical drive. They also consume less power because there is no need to power a motor to move mechanical parts. The benefits are obvious, but the speed and efficiency of SSD storage may not outweigh the current cost of the technology, which is roughly double the price per gigabyte of HDDs.

Figure 22. CompactFlash cards are a common type of storage for high-end devices.

Figure 23. SD cards are another type of common storge.

Figure 24. USB flash drives are one of the most commonly used storage devices.

Flash Memory

Solid-state drives use flash memory, which is faster and tends to last much longer than magnetic media because there are no moving parts. Many other types of flash devices also use flash memory.

CompactFlash (CF) is a flash memory device mainly used in portable electronic devices. Compact Flash remains popular today and is supported by many professional and high-end consumer devices like digital cameras and camcorders (Figure 22).

Secure Digital (SD) is a memory card format developed by the SD Card Association (SDA) for use in portable devices. **Secure Digital** includes four card families available in three different form factors, or shape and size standards (Figure 23). The four families are the original Standard-Capacity (SDSC), the High-Capacity (SDHC), the eXtended-Capacity (SDXC), and the Secure Digital Input Output (SDIO), which combines input and output functions with data storage. The three form factors are the original size, the mini, and the micro. Adapters will also allow the smaller cards to fit and function in a device built for a larger card. The SD card's small size is an ideal storage medium for small, thin, and portable electronic devices.

USB flash drives, also known as thumb drives, are a way of storing data on something lightweight, easy to carry, and easy to use. The universal serial bus (USB) connector works on all PC and Mac platforms. Every USB flash drive consists of a small printed circuit board, called a controller chip, that is connected to a flash memory module where the data are stored. Both elements are stored inside the drive's plastic, metal, or wood outer shell (Figure 24). The USB connector on the end of the flash drive is inserted into any PC or Mac. Data can then be read from or saved to the drive. USB flash drives don't need batteries because they draw the power they need from the USB port they are plugged into.

3. Output Hardware

Monitors

A monitor is a display device that outputs the visual information that a computer processes. It's the screen you look at when you use a computer. Monitors come in many types, but the CRT monitors of early desktop computers have mostly been replaced by LCD monitors today.

When comparing monitors, the number of pixels and the resolution size of the screen are most important. In digital imaging, a pixel — also referred to as a pel, or picture element — is a physical point in a rendered image. It is the smallest controllable element of a picture represented on the screen. The display resolution of a computer monitor signifies the number of distinct pixels in both width and height that can be displayed by the screen. Higher-end monitor models may be compared by looking at refresh rates in hertz, for which higher is better, and latency rates in milliseconds, for which lower is better.

CRT monitors use a cathode ray tube (CRT), which is a vacuum tube containing one or more electron guns that shoot light onto a phosphorescent screen used to view images (Figure 25). These monitors are heavy and take up more space than flat-panel displays. Due to their relatively high concentration of lead and phosphors, they are also considered one of the hardest types of electronics to recycle. As a result, CRTs are not very common today.

Figure 25. A traditional CRT monitor.

A **liquid-crystal display** (LCD) is usually a flat-panel visual display that uses liquid crystals to create an image. Liquid crystals do not emit light directly like CRT electron guns. Instead, they require external light to produce a visible image. In a transmissive type of LCD, this light is behind the glass "stack" of the screen and is called the backlight. LCDs are a more recent development, and because they have become more affordable, they have widely replaced CRTs. LCDs, in addition to being smaller and lighter than CRTs, use less energy and generate less heat (Figure 26).

Figure 26. An LCD monitor.

A **light-emitting diode** (LED) display is a flat panel that uses its diodes as pixels in a video display of potentially massive size. This capacity for large-scale images — as well as the extreme brightness of the image — makes this type of display a popular choice for outdoor signs and billboards to project video. They are also used for concerts and stage productions.

An **organic light-emitting diode** (OLED) display is a type of LED display whose light is produced by a very thin layer of organic compounds. They are popular as display panels in notebook computers due to their minimal thickness. They can also be used in

Figure 27. A dot-matrix printer.

Figure 28. A line printer.

Figure 29. An open ink-jet printer.

Figure 30. A laser printer and photocopier combo.

bendable displays, which means they can be used in unconventional ways, like with clothing. One of the biggest weaknesses of OLED displays, though, is that they do not last as long as conventional LED displays.

A **Retina display** is used in smartphones and some computers to smooth the edges of pixels in order to create smoother and less "pixelated" text and images. The technology was pioneered by Apple —the term "Retina display" is an Apple marketing term rather than a generic term — with the iPhone 4, but it can now be found in most modern smartphones, many tablets, and some laptop and desktop monitors.

The current frontier for home theater and computer displays is **4K resolution**. This refers to a horizontal resolution of 4000 pixels. 4K resolution can be achieved through the use of a variety of technologies, but the end result is previously unimaginable clarity.

Printers

Another common output device is a printer, which uses digital information to create physical marks on paper. Most printers can now print both images and text. Printers have benefited from a great deal of technological progress in recent years.

Dot-matrix printing, or impact matrix printing, is an old and increasingly rare type of computer printing which uses a print head that moves back and forth or up and down on the page (Figure 27). It prints by impact, striking an ink-soaked cloth ribbon against the paper, much like the keys on a typewriter would do. A **line printer** is an impact computer printer that prints one entire line of text at a time. It is mostly associated with punch-card equipment and the early days of electronic computing, but the technology is still occasionally in use (Figure 28).

A **color ink-jet** printer does a good job printing photos and other images in color using four colors of ink — cyan, magenta, yellow, and black, but the text it prints is often less crisp than that of a laser printer (Figure 29).

Laser printers print very crisp text. Cheaper models can only print in black and white and are good for environments like offices where high printing speed is needed (Figure 30). More expensive models can also print in color using the same four colors as a color ink-jet printer.

Figure 31. An LED printer.

Figure 32. A thermal printer.

Figure 33. A pen-plotter in action.

An **LED printer** is a type of computer printer similar to a laser printer. The light-emitting diode (LED) bar pulse-flashes across the entire page width and creates an image on the print drum or belt as it moves past. LEDs are more efficient and reliable than conventional laser printers because they have fewer moving parts, allowing for less mechanical wear (Figure 31).

Thermal printing, or direct thermal printing, is a digital printing process which produces a printed image by selectively heating coated thermochromic paper, commonly known as thermal paper, when the paper passes over the thermal print head (Figure 32). The coating turns black in the areas where it is heated, producing an image.

Figure 34. An electrostatic plotter.

A **plotter** is a computer printer for printing vector graphics. In the past, plotters were used in applications such as computer-aided design, but they have generally been replaced by wide-format conventional printers. A plotter uses a pen-like device to draw images on paper, producing a vector image hard copy of the otherwise screen-only output. Plotters are used to print designs of ships, buildings, and other large-scale objects. The two types of plotters are pen and electronic.

Figure 35. A 3D printer.

Pen plotters print by moving a pen or other instrument across the surface of a piece of paper (Figure 33). Pen plotters can draw complex line art, including text, but they do this slowly because of the mechanical movement of the pens. They are often incapable of efficiently creating a solid region of color, but can hatch an area by drawing a number of close, regular lines. **Electrostatic plotters** are most frequently used for computer-aided engineering (CAE). They produce raster images, which are pixels arranged within a set rectangular grid, using a liquid toner (Figure 34).

The only printing process described here that doesn't print onto paper, **3D printing**, creates a three-dimensional object from a computer model. A 3D printer is actually a type of industrial robot that deposits "elemental inks" to create the object (Figure 35).

Figure 36. An image projector.

Figure 37. USB computer speakers.

Figure 38. A humanoid robot.

Other Output Devices

An image **projector** is an optical device that projects an image or moving images onto a flat surface such as a wall or a projection screen (Figure 36). A projector's ability to display images is measured in lumens, which are the total quantity of visible light emitted by the light source. The higher the lumens, the better the projector's ability to project visible light on a surface. Projectors with high enough lumens can effectively project images on a screen even when a room is not darkened.

A **digital light processor** (DLP) is a type of digital video projector that uses micro-mirrors to reflect color and light onto a screen. DLP front projectors are primarily standalone projection units used in classrooms and businesses. DLP technology is also used in rear-projection televisions, some digital signs and billboards, and in most movie theaters that use digital projection equipment.

Computer speakers, or multimedia speakers, are used to project sound from computers. Most standalone computer speakers have an internal amplifier that requires an external power supply, batteries, or a USB port (Figure 37). A subwoofer, or sub, is an additional speaker that is dedicated to reproducing only the low-pitched audio frequencies known as bass.

Speech synthesis is the artificial production of human speech. A computer system used for this purpose is called a speech computer or speech synthesizer, and can be set up with either software or hardware. A text-to-speech (TTS) system converts normal language text into speech.

A **robot** is a mechanical or virtual artificial agent, usually an electro-mechanical machine that is guided by a computer program or electronic circuitry. Robots can be autonomous or semi-autonomous (Figure 38).

4. Connecting Hardware to a Computer

For the motherboard to interact with any input, storage, or output device, the motherboard and the device have to be connected. Computer developers and device developers follow industry standards for these connections to make sure that these interactions are reliable and efficient.

Universal Serial Bus

Universal Serial Bus (USB) is an industry standard that defines the design and operations of cables, connectors, power supply, and communication protocols for a **bus**, which is a communication system that transfers data between components within a computer, between computers, or between external devices and a computer (Figure 39).

Released in 1996, USB 1.0 specified data rates of 1.5 MB per second in Low Bandwidth or Low Speed and 12 MB per second in Full Bandwidth or Full Speed. Few USB devices actually made it to market, however, until USB 1.1 was released in 1998. USB 1.1 fixed problems that were discovered in USB 1.0 related to using hubs.

Figure 39. A standard Type A USB cable.

USB 2.0 was released in 2000, adding a higher maximum signaling rate of 480 MB per second called High Speed in addition to the USB 1 Full Speed rate of 12 MB per second. Because of access constraints on computer buses, however, the effective rate of USB 2.0 is limited to speeds of 35 MB per second or 280 MB per second.

The USB 3.0 standard was released in 2008, and it defined a new SuperSpeed mode of 5 GB per second. The USB 3.1 standard increased the data rate to 10 GB per second in the USB 3.1 Gen2 mode, double that of USB 3.0. The first use of USB 3.1 demonstrated transfer speeds of 7.2 GB per second. A USB 3.0 port is backward-compatible with USB 2.0 devices and cables.

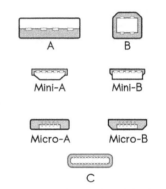

Figure 40. Each type (A and B) of USB comes in standard, mini, and micro sizes.

USB has two standard types, each with three sizes. **USB Type A** is available in standard, mini-A, and micro-A. **USB Type B** is available in in standard, mini-B, and micro-B (Figure 40). In 2014, **USB Type C** 1.0 was introduced. It's not necessarily compatible with USB 3.1. USB-C is meant as a replacement for USB-A and USB-B and is optimistically being touted as "future-proof." Adapters are necessary to connect USB-C to a device that uses one of the previous standards.

A **USB hub** is a device that expands a single USB port into several, so more ports are available to connect devices to a system (Figure 41). USB devices and hubs can be plugged into a computer without turning the computer off and on again. This ability is called "hot-swapping," and it makes USB compatibility more valuable for modern computer users. Once appropriate software is installed on the computer, a user can plug and unplug the component without restarting the computer.

Figure 41. A USB hub turns a single USB port into several ports.

Another interface standard is parallel ATA (**PATA**), which is derived from the earlier AT or ATA attachment standard. PATA cables can only be a maximum of 18 inches long, which limits their use to internal computer storage interface. This standard was renamed to differentiate it from serial ATA (SATA), which is now much more popular.

A video graphics array (**VGA**) connector, along with the generally compatible **DVI** standard, enjoyed widespread use for video cards, monitors, laptops, projectors, and HD TV sets until fairly recently. Now, however, it is more common to find high-definition multimedia interface (**HDMI**) connectors due to their more compact size. First marketed in late 2003, HDMI is the current favorite for transmitting video and digital audio. Newer versions of HDMI have improved capacity, performance and resolution, but all forms of HDMI use the same cable and connector.

KVM Switch

Figure 42. A KVM swtich.

A **KVM switch** (an abbreviation for "keyboard, video and mouse") is a hardware device that allows a user to control multiple computers from one or more sets of keyboards, video monitors, and mice. Typically, more computers can be connected to the KVM at once than can actually be controlled at once. Currently, other peripherals like USB and audio devices can be shared via a KVM switch (Figure 42).

Other Types of Connections

FireWire (IEEE 1394) is an interface standard for high-speed communications and real-time data transfer. The FireWire interface is comparable to USB, but FireWire connections of several devices require the presence of an electrical signal "terminator" in the last device in the chain to prevent electrical interference. This added requirement makes FireWire less user-friendly and is likely the reason that USB has become more popular in consumer products (Figure 43).

Figure 43. A FireWire connection cable.

Thunderbolt is the brand name of a hardware interface that allows the connection of external peripherals to a computer (Figure 44). Thunderbolt combines PCI Express (PCIe) and DisplayPort (DP) into one serial signal, and additionally provides DC power, all in one cable. Three versions of Thunderbolt have been created, and each generation has added increased speed and versatility. Version 1 offered 10 gigabits per channel or 20 gigabits per second total. Version 2 offered 20 one-gigabit channels or 20 gigabits per second total. Version 3 offered 40 gigabits per second.

Figure 44. A thunderbolt or lightning cable.

Serial AT Attachment (**SATA**) is a computer bus interface that connects the motherboard bus adapters to storage devices like hard disk drives, optical drives, and solid-state drives. Internal SATA devices are connected via a standard SATA plug for data and a separate standard power plug. Both the data and power plugs are L-shaped, making them easily recognizable as SATA plugs. As a result, connecting multiple SATA drives in a single computer system is relatively simple. The external plug variety of SATA connectors, called eSATA, is widely used for connecting external hard drives (Figure 45). Three versions of SATA have been created, and each uses Roman numerals to avoid confusion with the similar numbers for the data transfer speed in each. SATA-I offers 1.5 gigabits (150 MB) per second. SATA-II offers 3 gigabits (300 MB) per second. SATA-III offers 6.0 gigabits (600 MB) per second.

Small Computer System Interface (SCSI) is an older set of standards for physically connecting and transferring data between computers and peripheral devices. The SCSI standards define commands, communication protocols, and electrical and optical interfaces. SCSI is mostly out of use now, having been replaced by SATA as the method most commonly used for hard disk drives and tape drives (Figure 46). SCSI can connect a wide range of other devices, including scanners and CD drives, but not all controllers can handle all devices.

Wireless devices can transfer information or otherwise communicate without a physical connection. This term describes many wireless technologies beyond computers, including radio and television waves. Common wireless technologies used with computers include Wi-Fi and Bluetooth. **WIFI, Wi-Fi,** and **WiFi** are interchangeable terms for a local area wireless computer networking technology that allows electronic devices to connect to a network. In Chapter 5, "Communication Networks," we describe networks in more detail. **Bluetooth** is a wireless technology standard for exchanging data over short distances from stationary and mobile devices. The proximity feature of Bluetooth — you must be within a specific signal distance to connect — helps define Bluetooth networks as personal area networks.

Figure 45. A SATA cable.

Figure 46. A SCSI connector.

A **dongle** is a small piece of hardware that connects with another device to provide it with additional functionality (Figure 47). The term is associated with devices meant to provide additional forms of wireless connectivity to other devices like the ones that Wi-Fi or Bluetooth support, often over USB connections. These devices can also connect personal computers to media players like Amazon Fire TV Stick, Chromecast, and Roku Streaming Stick. The term "dongle" is also associated with hardware that provides a copy-protection mechanism for commercial software. For example, in order for certain software to function, a dongle must be attached to the system on which the software is installed.

Figure 47. A Bluetooth dongle that connects via USB.

Chapter 3
File Management

File management is how you and your computer organize information for easy retrieval. Information is stored in files, and file management arranges those files in folders — also known as directories — on your computer's hard drive. By storing folders within other folders, file management creates a hierarchical file system (HFS) that arranges information by order of importance or scope. At the top of the hierarchy is the hard drive itself. Under the drive, you have the main folders. Under those main folders are subfolders or files.

Figure 1. An example of a file icon, specifically for a text file.

It's important to sort files properly into folders so that you can find your files again. It's not uncommon for students to have to redo entire projects because the files they were working on were saved in the wrong folder. The same problem happens in the business world, too.

In order to understand how file management works, we first have to define some of the key components of the file-management system. **Files** are the most basic collections of data and information. A file can store the instructions for a single program or the data for a single letter, so file size varies widely (Figure 1). **Folders** are collections of files (Figure 2). You can think of a file as a piece of paper that you put into a manila folder. A single folder can hold many pieces of paper.

You can think of file management as an upside-down tree. The drive is the main root or trunk of the tree, the folders are the limbs that are connected to that trunk, and the files are the branches and leaves connected to those limbs (Figure 3).

Figure 2. A folder icon.

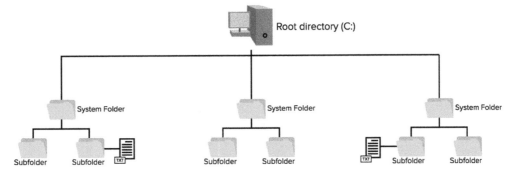

Figure 3. Basic file system.

In this chapter, we'll look at how file management works for both Windows and Mac computers. You'll find that with both systems, a few simple techniques will help you to keep your information organized and easy to retrieve.

1. Windows File Management

On a Windows PC, the storage and organization of files and folders follows structural rules that hold true across different versions. The root is typically the C: drive, which is the first hard disk boot partition. Drives D: through Z: are other disk partitions. Windows assigns the next free drive letter to the next drive it encounters while spelling out the disk drives on the system. These basics apply to most recent versions of Windows, including XP, Vista, 7, 8, and 10. The titles of some programs have changed, but they offer the same basic functionality described here.

Figure 4.

Figure 5.

Windows doesn't start with the lettered drives A: and B: because those lettered drives were traditionally reserved for floppy disks. This goes back to a time when PCs didn't have hard drives and needed to boot up from a floppy drive. The A: drive was for 3.5" or 5.25" floppy disks — and possibly other types of removable disk drives such as ZIP drives (Figure 4) and (Figure 5). The B: drive was reserved for a second floppy drive, if present. It was not uncommon to have a 3.5 and a 5.25 floppy drive on the same computer.

In versions of Windows through Windows 7, the central place to manage files located in multiple locations on your computer was through libraries. Libraries are the main folders on the hard disk. Since Windows 8.1, libraries have been replaced by File Explorer — although libraries can still be turned on in Windows 10. The main libraries in Windows are Documents, Downloads, Music, Pictures, and Videos, and users can add their own favorites to the libraries menu (Figure 6).

File Explorer is the file-manager application previously called Windows Explorer in versions of Windows through Windows 7. File Explorer and Windows Explorer are included as parts of the Windows operating system. Each provides a graphical user interface (GUI) for accessing file systems on your computer. When you have a folder or library open, you can navigate its contents by using these navigation tools embedded into the File Explorer window (Figure 7).

Figure 6. File Explorer with various libraries on the left.

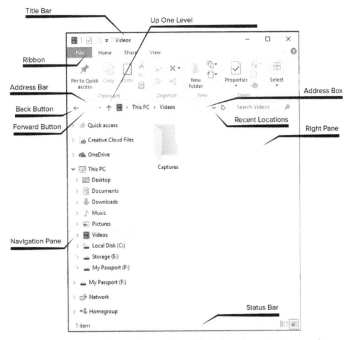

Figure 7. Windows File Explorer labeled with navigation tools.

Title Bar	Displays the name and location of the library. Also includes some navigation tools, such as "minimize," and "close" buttons.
Ribbon	Contains tabs with buttons and other tools for managing files.
Address Bar	Includes tools for displaying folder contents and finding files.
Navigation Pane	Lists other available drives and folders by icon, usually based on frequently used locations.
Right Pane	Displays icons for actual files and folders
Status Bar	Below the right pane, displays information about the selected locations and files.
File Extension	Most files named with two parts. The first part of the filename is a description of the file. After this comes a period, followed by the second part. The second part of a filename is claled the extension. Extensions are often three letters long and they tell you what kind of file you're dealing with. For example, files with an "exe" extension are programs and files with a "doc" or "docx" extension are Microsoft Word documents.

Table 1. File Explorer navigation options.

Once you have displayed your folders, you can work with them and navigate the folders to find and relocate specific files. These tools help you navigate your folders (Table 2):

Back button	Return to the previous loction from your current screen.
Forward button	Available only after you have used the back button, reversing the process and returning you to your last screen before you clicked back.
Recent locations button	Navigate to a location you've visited since you opened File Explorer.
Up one level button	Navigate to the folder that contains the current folder.
Address box	Displays your current folder as a series of folder names spearated by arrow buttons. Click any other folder to navigate up to its level.

Table 2. More navigation tools.

Figure 8. Windows 10 desktop, with start menu opened.

Components of the Windows Desktop

The desktop is the area that appears on your screen immediately after you log into a user account. The desktop is a conceptual metaphor for the real desk top that you might use to do your homework or fill out a job application — a place where you might have folders and files to work with. A computer desktop contains a background picture known as wallpaper and small images called icons that represent programs, folders, and files (Figure 8). At the bottom of the desktop is a taskbar.

By default, the **taskbar** sits horizontally on the bottom of the desktop. It can also be moved to the top or either side of the desktop. The taskbar is used for launching programs or viewing the window of an open program (Figure 9). On one side of the taskbar is a clock, and beside the clock are several icons that represent open but "invisible" programs. These are programs that are always running and do things behind the scenes, making them invisible

Figure 9. Windows 10 taskbar.

Figure 10. Mac OS taskbar.

Figure 11. Windows 10 with the quick launch toolbar on the left-hand side of the screen.

Figure 12. Recycle bins for both Windows (left) and Mac (right).

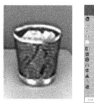

Figure 13. Windows 10 start menu.

to the user. This area of the taskbar is called the system tray. You'll find tray icons for things like wireless connection, sound features like volume, and any background programs like antivirus or cloud storage systems that don't require regular maintaining or opening by the user (Figure 10).

Part of the system tray is the **notification area**, a small triangle that, when clicked, reveals more icons that notify users of available updates or system messages that need attention. The group of larger icons on the main part of the taskbar is called the **quick launch toolbar** (Figure 11). Clicking on one of the icons within it opens whatever program or file that the icon represents. You can also press the Windows button and a number representing the order in which the shortcut sits in the Quick Launch list. For example, pressing [windows icon] +2 will open the second program in the list. If you accidentally delete a file you wanted to keep, you can open the **recycle bin** by double-clicking on its desktop icon, then right-clicking on the file and selecting "restore" from the pop-up menu. If you want to permanently get rid of all files in the recycle bin, right-click on the recycle bin and select "empty recycle bin" from the pop-up menu. Options for deleting or restoring folders are contained within this same menu (Figure 12).

On the opposite side of the taskbar from the clock, you'll find the start button. When left-clicked, this icon opens the **start menu** (Figure 13). When right-clicked, it opens a menu with administrative tools and shutdown options (Figure 14). The Windows 10 start button is a blend of the old Windows 7 menu and the often-reviled Windows 8 Start screen. This menu contains icons for installed programs and data collections. Typically, most of these icons are for programs. When opened, the start menu shows your computer's frequently opened programs and any that you have chosen to "pin" to the start menu, making them visible near the top of the menu's left side. Below that, you'll also find areas to open all available programs — labeled, logically enough, "All Programs" — and to search for files and folders by name.

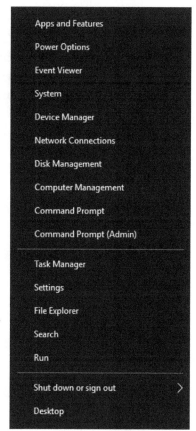

Figure 14. Windows 10 Start Menu after right-click.

On the right side of the start menu, you'll find links to other libraries so that you can quickly navigate to the main folders and subfolders where most of your files are stored. You'll also find links to the control panel, device management menus, and help-and-support tutorials and services. Finally, the start menu contains the buttons to shut down, restart, sleep, hibernate, lock, and log off of Windows.

2. Apple OS File Management

The file system used for MacOS and iOS is HFS Plus, which is a UNIX-based hierarchical file structure. Just like Windows, it stores files within folders. The top folder is known as the root directory. Folders located in or beneath the root directory are known as subfolders or subdirectories — two ways of saying the same thing. However, the HFS Plus Mac file system also supports a variety of other formats, including the Windows File Allocation Table (FAT) and New Technology File System (NTFS). This means that on a Mac, you should be able to view a flash drive of folders and documents that were created on a Windows computer.

Finder, which is similar to Windows Explorer, is the user's main point of access to the file system in MacOS. You get to the Finder by clicking anywhere on the Apple desktop or selecting its smiling icon from the Dock (Figure 15).

Finder uses windows and icons to show the content of the Mac. The sidebar in a Finder window contains shortcuts to AirDrop, commonly used folders, and iCloud Drive, plus devices such as hard drives, documents, applications, downloads, and more. It also includes your home folder, which is identified by a little house icon and your short username. Items in the sidebar open with just one click.

You can configure the Finder window to illustrate file structure in three different ways.

Figure 15. Finder icon.

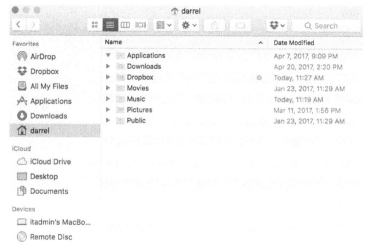

Figure 16. Finder window using list view.

Figure 17. Finder with column view.

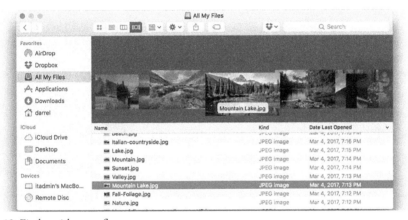

Figure 18. Finder with cover flow.

The list view shows details about folders such as the size, type of file, and date the file or folder was last modified. Folders have small triangles next to them. If you click on a triangle, the folder expands to show you the contents of that folder. You can expand and manipulate more than one folder this way (Figure 16).

The **column view** shows the contents of the current folder and highlights the folder or folders that contain it (Figure 17). If you select a file, you will also see information about that file and a preview of the file. You can widen columns by dragging the lines that separate them.

The cover-flow view is based on the way that iTunes and iPhones display album covers to help you find the music files that you want. In the Finder, the cover-flow view shows a preview of a file's contents. If you click on the highlighted image at the top of the window (or press the spacebar), you will see a readable, scrollable preview of the center file (Figure 18).

Components of the Mac Desktop

The Mac desktop contains eight elements (Figure 19). At the top is the Menu bar, which contains the first six of those eight elements. The seventh element is the desktop space itself, the main body of the computer screen. At the bottom of the screen, the eight element is the Dock.

In the menu bar (element 3) at the top of the screen, the Apple menu (element 1) provides access to software updates, system preferences, and the Apple store. This menu also allows you to shut down your computer, restart it, or put it into sleep mode.

Next to the Apple menu is the application menu (element 2). This menu contains the menus for any application you are using and changes as you shift from one application to another. The name of the application appears next to the Apple menu. Then application menus appear to the right of the application name.

The status menu (element 4) shows the status of the date and time, Bluetooth connections, sound, Wi-Fi, and other information. Each icon also provides quick access to that feature. For example, you can use it to open the system preferences for sound or Wi-Fi and change those settings.

The Spotlight icon (element 5) brings up the Spotlight search field. If you click on this icon, it will open the Spotlight search bar. You can use this to search for any file or folder on your computer. From there, you can open the file or have Spotlight show you where the file is located on your computer.

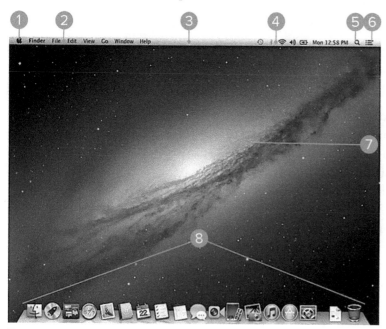

The notification center menu (element 6) consolidates notifications from Messages, Calendar, Mail, Reminders, and other third-party apps. You can also configure the notifications center to consolidate current information about weather, stocks, and news articles.

At the bottom of the screen is the Dock (element 8), but you can move the Dock to either side of the screen if you prefer. There are two parts to the Dock. The left-hand side — or top if your Dock is on a side of the screen — provides

Figure 19. Mac OS desktop.

shortcut icons to applications and system software. You can drag icons off the Dock to remove them. You can also drag applications onto the Dock to add shortcut icons. The right-hand side — or bottom — provides shortcuts for trash, downloads, documents, minimized windows, and any files or folders you drag onto the Dock. The Dock works in the same way that the Quick Launch bar does in Windows.

File Management Practices

No matter if you are using a PC, a Mac, or a Linux computer, you should follow good file management practices. The ability to locate your files when you need them is an essential skill for anyone who uses a computer. And when you have a paper due in five minutes and need to find the file on your computer, it's even more important. The following practices will help you manage your files effectively.

1. Store your file in one place. Both Windows and Mac have default folders for documents, pictures, videos, and downloads. Saving files to the corresponding folder that best describes the file is a good step towards organization.

2. Don't overdo subfolders. Subfolders are useful for organizing your files. However, be conscious of how many folders-within-folders you have, because opening folder after folder looking for your files can be a daunting task. Create your folders in a logical hierarchy so that files and subfolders are smaller divisions of the folders that contain them. Don't group unrelated projects or files. An example of good file management would be having your School folder in the Documents folder and a folder for each subject inside the School folder (Figure 20).

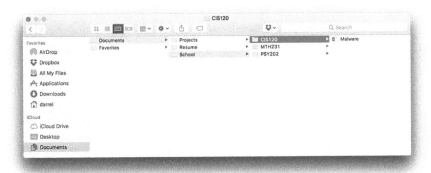

Figure 20. Folder organization examples.

3. Follow naming conventions. Name your related documents in a similar way, such as "Essay2_Draft1" and "Essay2_Draft2." You should also name your files so that you know what they are without opening them. For example, don't name a file for your computer class "CIS.docx." Give it a more descriptive name, such as "Malware_Overview.docx."

4. Don't use spaces in your file names. Some operating systems, such as MacOS, allow the use of spaces in file names. Other operating systems do not. If you transfer files between different operating systems, use an underscore instead of a space to avoid any problems. A space signifies the end of a text string, so spaces in a file name can complicate file searches. Spaces are also frequently translated in a web environment to be read as "%20." This alteration causes confusion in identifying the actual file name. For example, a file called "File naming tutorial.docx" appears as: "File%20naming%20tutorial.docx" when the file is available online.

5. Keep file names under 25 characters. Both Windows and MacOS allow for file names of up to 255 characters. Generally, though, about 25 characters will capture enough information for describing a document.

6. Cull your files. "Cull" means to reduce or control the size of a group of things by removing unneeded or unwanted parts of the group. Cleaning out files that you no longer need reduces clutter and frees up space on your hard drive for more important files.

7. Archive files. You can also archive folders and files you want to keep but are not immediately using. Archiving compresses the file so it will take up less space on your hard drive. In Windows, right-click on the file or folder and from the Context menu select Send to Compressed (zipped) folder. In MacOS, right-click on the file or folder and from the context menu select Compress.

8. Back up your files. Maintaining good backup practices helps ensure that you never accidentally delete a file that you may actually need. This could be as simple as syncing your files to a "cloud-based" storage system such as OneDrive, which comes with Microsoft Office, or iCloud, which comes with MacOS. Apple also offers Time Machine, which can be set up to sync with a Wi-Fi-based storage solution or an external hard drive.

Chapter 4
Computer Software

Computer software is a broad term that includes all the programs, procedures, and algorithms that a computer uses while operating. Unlike the hardware in Chapter 2, software doesn't have a physical structure. You can't touch it the way you can touch a keyboard or hard drive or monitor. That's what puts the "soft" in software.

Software is more than just the computer's word-processing or gaming or web-browsing programs. Software also includes programs that provide instructions for a computer to perform tasks, as well as all the related data that are held, used, or created in any form of computer storage.

There are a wide variety of software types, from large-scale programs that provide the basis for using a computer at all to relatively small programs that let users do simple calculations on their own. This chapter will look at many kinds of software, from operating systems to different types of applications.

1. Operating Systems

The operating system is the most important software in any computing device. An operating system does so much that this chapter will only explore the surface of all its different functions. In short, the operating system manages the hardware and software systems for your computer. You might be thinking, "But that's everything!" If that's what you're thinking, then you're right.

When you turn on a computer, it boots up. In the course of this process, the operating system chooses which programs, functions, features, and information to make available at startup. Organizing and managing files also happens within the operating system, and so does managing security operations like logging in, maintaining firewalls, and managing user permissions. Whenever you are operating your computer, in other words, you are working within the parameters of the operating system. Just imagine how complex the system must be to do all that.

Fortunately, the operating system's real job is to make it easier for you to operate your computer without needing extensive technical knowledge. Common operating systems on personal computers include Windows, Mac OS, and Linux, but operating systems exist on more than just personal computers. They are on any machine that runs multiple applications and allows users to interact with it.

Types of Interfaces

An operating system provides the space — called an interface — for users to give instructions for the computer to process. There are three main types of interface — the graphical user interface (GUI), the command-line interface (CLI), and embedded systems.

The **GUI** (pronounced "gooey") is a visual interface that many users prefer because of its simplicity. A GUI tends to be visually appealing in a way that makes users want to interact with it (Figure 1). In a GUI, performing simple tasks like opening files involves clicking on a visual icon, dragging a folder across a visual space, or right-clicking files and navigating through choices presented in a visual list. Chapter 3 showed you how file management works with two GUI systems — Windows and Apple's Mac OS.

The **CLI** is a text-based interface that uses typed commands to perform tasks (Figure 2). Disk operating systems (DOS) are operating systems that only use the CLI. Most operating systems include a CLI as an optional alternative to their standard GUI. The CLI can accomplish many of the same things as a GUI, but it requires users to know the CLI language to run commands. Having to know a wide variety of commands may be the reason why many users are scared by the idea of using the CLI. Still, users can create folders, navigate through them, view files, adjust settings, encrypt files, and perform many more operations, using only typed commands.

In Windows, the CLI is called the **Command Prompt**. In Mac OS, the CLI is called **Terminal**. On computers using Linux operating systems, the CLI varies depending on which version of Linux is used. Common Linux CLIs include BASH, zsh, and Konsole. **Network utilities** provide commands that function as basic tools for troubleshooting network communication problems. One common type is the IPCONFIG utility that tests whether your computer is connected to the Internet via your local network. IPCONFIG is a CLI command that lets you configure ("CONFIG") the Internet provider ("IP") addresses for your network. Another common network utility is PING, which tests the reachability of a host on an IP network, "pinging" that host and measuring the time, usually in milliseconds (ms), that it takes to get a response.

Figure 1. Ubuntu (a common Linux-based OS) desktop interface.

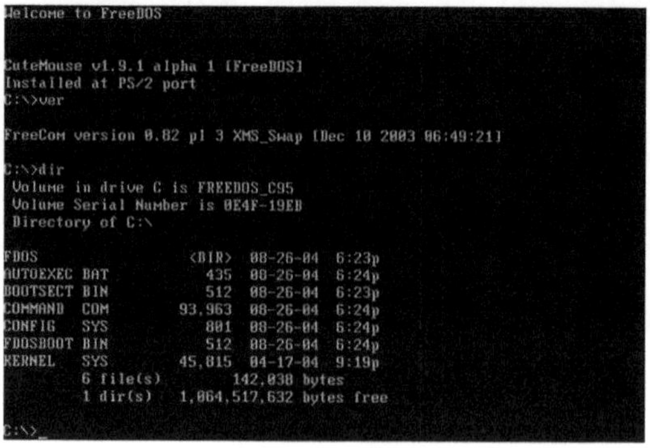

Figure 2. Example of a CLI interface.

Embedded operating systems are found in machines and computers with specialized, narrow purposes, like automobiles, ATMs, routers, mobile phones, smartphones, and digital media players (Figure 3). These operating systems are designed to be compact, efficient, and reliable. Having fewer parts means there is a lower likelihood of failure, so these systems don't include many functions that GUI and CLI computer operating systems provide (Figure 4).

Figure 3. Mobile devices have their own embedded operating system.

Operating System Software

System software refers to all the files and programs that are not required for the operating system to function but that expand or improve its basic functionality for the user. When you install the operating system, the system software is installed with it. Some system software ensures that the computer can perform basic functions, allowing it to run other programs that rely on those functions.

Figure 4. Modern cars use an embedded operating system.

Device drivers are programs that enable a computer's operating system to communicate with parts of its hardware that do not use a common standard for communication. Since there are so many different types of monitors, modems, network cards, and printers that need to communicate with the operating system, drivers connect to the operating system by communicating with the hardware in a way the operating system can understand. Hardware that uses a recognized standard for communicating with the operating system, such as processors, RAM, and USB drives, does not need a driver.

Device drivers are typically provided by the manufacturer of the hardware, or may come pre-installed in your computer's operating system. The support website for the manufacturer of the hardware, or for the manufacturer of the computer if the hardware was original equipment, is generally a good place to find information on relevant drivers or to download new drivers if necessary.

A **software library** is a collection of files and programming code that support a software application. In Windows programming, the software library is called a **dynamic-link library** (DLL). In Java programming, it's called a **Java Archive** (JAR). These files are used to develop software programs and applications, and they are included with the application itself because they contain functions and resources that the software applications use to perform particular tasks. They're designed to assist both the programmer and the programming-language compiler. For example, when writing an Internet application, a programmer might include an existing security library to avoid writing the complex code needed for a brand-new security function in the application.

Besides the basic commands associated with network utilities, users wishing to trouble-shoot their computers also have access to the **utility software** integrated into most operating systems. This software includes tools to uninstall programs, clean up and defragment disk drives, and restore your system after a failure. Regardless of the name, which is specific to each operating system, utility software generally functions the same.

2. Application Software

Application software refers to the programs that allow you to open, change, save, or create a file on your computer. Applications can be anything from word processors to video games to media players to web browsers (Figure 5). This chapter will look first at the ways software licenses define how applications can be used. Then it will look more closely at different types of applications.

Figure 5. A variety of different application software.

Software Licenses

A **software license** states the software publisher's rights, the allowed conditions for using the software, and the user's permission to use the software. You can think of a software license as a contract that defines the limits of your rights to use the software. You must sign that contract — agree to the license — to be allowed to use the software.

Most users do not read these license agreements, which appear during the first few steps of installing a new program. However, the information is extremely important, especially because ignorance of the rules doesn't mean the rules don't apply to you. They do. The rights to use, copy, alter, and distribute the software are especially important. Some programs may only allow you to install them once on only one computer, while others may allow you a certain number of installs before prohibiting any more. Distributing the software to others, or sharing it, could mean breaking the license agreement and could even terminate the availability of the software.

There are three main types of software licenses in use today. It's important to know what kind of license your software has so that you don't use the software beyond the agreement's limits.

Retail software, or commercial software, is developed and sold for profit by the developer. Its licenses have the strictest limits for use. If you have purchased or licensed the software before using it, be sure to know how the license defines its use.

Shareware is software that you can obtain for free on a limited trial basis. It may also be found pre-installed on new computers that have commercial operating systems already installed on them. If you wish to keep the software after the trial basis, you are required to pay a small fee. It is sometimes possible to use shareware after the trial period ends, but this is an unethical use of the software because it violates the license agreement.

Freeware is software that does not require the user to pay anything because the copyright owner has expressly released compensation rights for using the software. However, the copyright owner keeps ownership of the software. The owner is the only one who can sell, distribute, or modify it, but there are no time limits or other usage restrictions on the software.

Types of Software

There are as many types of application software as there are tasks to perform. In this section, we'll introduce some of the main types of software you are likely to use.

Productivity Software

Software applications that allow users to create, modify, and publish documents for personal or professional use are called **productivity software**. These are sometimes available in "suites" — groups of related programs that often pass information to and from each other. For example, a spreadsheet might allow you open its data in a slide creator for displaying a table in a presentation.

Two widely used suites are **Microsoft Office** and **Apache OpenOffice**. Microsoft Office is a software suite of programs that includes Word for word processing, Excel for spreadsheet creation, PowerPoint for presentation software, Access for database management, and Outlook for email communication — among other programs. Apache OpenOffice is a suite of similar programs that is available as freeware. While many of the same features as Microsoft Office are available for free in OpenOffice, other key features are not, so Microsoft Office tends to be a more frequent choice for businesses and professional organizations.

Graphics Software

Software applications that allow the user to create and manipulate image files are called **graphics software**. With the rise of affordable image-capturing technology, graphics software has become more and more widely available to consumers.

Adobe Photoshop is a "raster graphics editor" application. Raster images are data structures that use a rectangular grid of pixels. Photoshop includes specific image-editing tools and a user-friendly interface. The program allows users to edit and retouch image files and includes tools for free-form drawing, resizing, cropping, creating photo-montages, converting files between different image formats, and performing more specialized tasks. Adobe, the software's publisher, publishes large suites of professional-grade digital art and design software.

A less expensive version of Photoshop, called **Adobe Photoshop Elements**, is sold with several of the more advanced features turned off, making it more manageable for average users. **GIMP** (GNU Image Manipulation Program) is a free and open-source raster graphics editor that is similar to Photoshop but with fewer features.

Audio Software

Audio applications let users create and edit audio files, and they are becoming more widely available because of the rise of affordable audio-capturing technology. Popular applications include Pro Tools, Garage Band, and Audacity.

Pro Tools is a digital audio workstation that lets audio engineers record, mix, and master audio signals from live or digital sources in a digital audio file format. Like all digital audio workstation software, Pro Tools is similar to a multi-track tape recorder and mixer, but comes with additional features that can only be performed digitally. Pro Tools supports multiple audio sampling rates and file sizes, and can work with several file types, including WAV, AIFF, AIFC, mp3, Windows Media Audio (WMA), and QuickTime video files. Pro Tools features time code, tempo maps, elastic audio, automation, and surround sound abilities.

GarageBand is a software application that comes pre-installed with Mac OS and iOS. Its music and podcast creation system lets users create multiple tracks with pre-made MIDI keyboards, pre-made loops, voice recordings, and an array of instrumental effects. The pre-made feature means these instruments and effects can be created without live sound inputs. GarageBand supports many sound formats, with the exception of mp3 or any formats at 8-bit sample rate or lower. It is a less professional grade of audio engineering software than Pro Tools, but its features are much easier to use without an audio engineering background, making it a more user-friendly example of audio software.

Audacity is a freeware audio application that offers many features of both Pro Tools and GarageBand but lacks such aspects as dynamic equalizer controls and real-time audio effects while recording. Audacity does not natively import or export WMA, AAC, AC3, or most other proprietary or restricted file formats. However, the free and open nature of Audacity has made it very popular in education, encouraging its developers to make the user interface easier for students and teachers. Since its release in 2000, it has been downloaded from freeware sites over 85 million times.

Antivirus Software

Antivirus software is computer software used to prevent, detect, and remove malicious software. Most of these programs perform the same functions, with each boasting about its effectiveness compared to the others. It's difficult to know precisely how effective your antivirus software will be, but it's important to have *something* in place to prevent harm to your computer's data.

Popular retail antivirus programs are available from Norton, McAfee, Kaspersky, and Trend Micro. Many come bundled with the programs initially installed on new computers or can be installed as shareware with other programs. These begin as free trials and then prompt users to pay a subscription fee to continue use. Not all these programs require paying a fee. Some of the most popular freeware antivirus programs are AVG, Panda, and BitDefender. While these programs are freeware, they are also available in retail versions with additional features.

More information about the importance and usefulness of antivirus software and other protection programs can be found in Chapter 8, "Security and Safety."

Chapter 5
Communication Networks

A computer network allows computers to exchange data. A network allows files, data, and information to be shared by giving authorized users access to these things stored on other computers on the network. This lets users communicate easily and efficiently using applications like email, instant messaging, chat rooms, telephone and video calls, and video conferencing. A network also allows computers to share network resources. Users may use resources provided by other devices on the network, such as the ability to print a document on a shared network printer.

Figure 1.

The best-known computer network is the Internet, which links millions of computers to one another, but as Table 1 illustrates, there are many more types of networks that make computer communication possible.

PAN (personal area network)	This is a network used for data transmission among devices such as computers, telephones, and other personal devices. PANs can be used for intrapersonal communication (communication among the personal devices themselves), or for uplinking (connecting to a higher-level network and to the Internet).
LAN (local area network)	This is a network that interconnects computers within a limited area like a residence, school, laboratory, or office building.
HAN (home area network)	This is a type of local area network that facilitates communication among digital devices inside or close to a user's home.
MAN (metro area network)	This is a computer network much larger than a local area network, covering an area varying from a few city blocks to an entire city and its surrounding area.
WAN (wide area network)	This is a telecommunications or computer network that extends over a large geographical distance. Wide area networks are often established with leased telecommunication circuits.
GAN (global area network)	This is a network composed of smaller interconnected computer networks and covering an unlimited geographical area.

SAN (storage area network)	This is a network that provides access to consolidated, block-level data storage, and is primarily used to enhance storage devices, such as disk arrays, tape libraries, and optical jukeboxes. SANs are accessible via servers so that the storage devices appear to the operating system as locally attached devices (Figure 2).
EPN (enterprise private network)	This is a computer network built by a business to interconnect its various company sites (such as production sites, offices, and shops) so they can share computer resources. Enterprise networks are now commonly referred to as enterprise private networks in order to clarify that they are not public networks for customers.
VPN (virtual private network)	This extends the reach of a private network across a public network, such as the Internet. It enables users to send and receive data across shared or public networks as if their computing devices were directly connected to the private network and benefiting from the functionality, security, and management policies of that private network (Figure 3).

Table 1. Types of networks.

As Table 2 illustrates, networks have evolved greatly over the past fifty years.

This chapter looks more closely at how networks operate. It begins by introducing the elements within a network. It then looks at how networks are structured and used for different purposes. The chapter ends by examining how communication occurs between computers and networks.

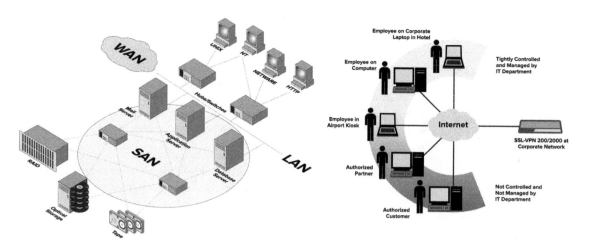

Figure 2. Diagram of a SAN network.

Figure 3. Diagram of a VPN network.

Late 1950s	Early networks of computers include the military radar system called Semi-Automatic Ground Environment (SAGE).
1959	The Soviet Union proposes a plan to reorganize the control of its armed forces and economy around a network of computing centers.
1960s	Development begins independently on three different network systems using packets to transfer information between computers over a network.
1960	A commercial airline reservation system, Semi-Automatic Business Research Environment (SABRE), comes online with two connected mainframes.
1962	Development begins on a workgroup called the "Intergalactic Computer Network" at the Advanced Research Projects Agency (ARPA).
1964	Researchers at Dartmouth College develop the Dartmouth Time Sharing System for distributed users of large computer systems.
1964	At Massachusetts Institute of Technology, a research group supported by General Electric and Bell Labs uses a computer to route and manage telephone connections.
1965	Thomas Marill and Lawrence G. Roberts create the first WAN.
1965	Western Electric introduces the first widely used telephone switch that implements true computer control.
1969	University of California at Los Angeles, the Stanford Research Institute, University of California at Santa Barbara, and University of Utah become connected using 50-kilobits-per-second circuits, forming the beginning of the ARPANET network.
1972	Commercial services using the X.25 network protocol are deployed, and are later used as an underlying infrastructure for expanding TCP/IP networks.
1976	Robert Metcalfe and David Boggs publish their paper "Ethernet: Distributed Packet Switching for Local Computer Networks" and collaborate on several patents.
1976	Datapoint Corporation creates ARCNET, a token-passing network first used to share storage devices.
1995	The transmission speed capacity for Ethernet increases from 10 Megabits per second to 100 Megabits per second.
1998	Ethernet supports transmission speeds of a Gigabit per second.
2016	Ethernet supports transmission speeds of 100 Gigabits per second.

Table 2. A brief history of networks.

1. Network Elements

In computer networks, networked devices exchange data with each other using a data link. The connections between links use either wired media — with cables — or wireless media. Networks complete these processes by sending and receiving information packets over links based on the network's topology or layout.

Network Packets

A network packet is a collection of data that can be transferred as a unit from device to device over a network. Rather than a continuous stream of individual bits of data, which would take much longer to send, packets are sent as groupings of data that are usually a few tens of bytes to a few kilobytes long. The majority of computers, including nearly all that have Internet access, are connected to a packet-switched network — a network that's capable of transmitting packets.

Packets consist of two kinds of data: control information and user data — also known as **payload**. The **control information** provides directions the network needs to deliver the user data. For example, source and destination network addresses, error detection codes, and sequencing information are all user data. Typically, control information is found in **packet headers** and **trailers**, and the payload data are in between.

Once the packets arrive at their destination, they are reassembled into their original message. With packets, bandwidth can be better shared among users. When one user is not sending packets, the link can be filled with packets traveling from other users. Often the route that a packet needs to take through a network is not immediately available. In that case, the packet is queued and waits until a link is free. This means many devices can share network bandwidth without complications as long as the data link isn't overused.

Network Links

There are many ways to create links within a network and between networks. These can be broken down into wired and wireless links. When distinguishing between these two options, price is a key factor. Going wireless means a higher price than for wired computers, printers, and other devices. However, some businesses have needs that can only be met by wireless technology and these may override cost considerations.

Wired Technologies

One popular form of wired technology is **coaxial cable,** which is widely used for cable television systems, office buildings, and other worksites that use local area networks (Figure 4). This type of cable consists of copper or aluminum wire surrounded by an insulating layer — typically a flexible material with a high dielectric constant — that is then surrounded by a conductive layer. The insulation helps to minimize interference and distortion. Transmission speed ranges from 200 million bits per second to more than 500 million bits per second. In a similar vein, **ITU-T G.hn** technology uses existing home wiring such as coaxial cable, phone lines, or power lines to create a high-speed local area network capable of transmitting up to 1 gigabit per second.

Figure 4. Inside a coaxial cable.

Twisted-pair wire is the most widely used medium for all telecommunication (Figure 5). Twisted-pair cabling consists of copper wires that are, not surprisingly, twisted into pairs. For ordinary telephone wires, the pairs of copper wires are insulated. Ethernet cables consist of four pairs of copper wires that can be used for both voice and data transmission. Using two wires twisted together helps reduce interference and electromagnetic heat. The transmission speed ranges from two megabits per second to 10 gigabits per second. Twisted-pair cabling comes in two forms — unshielded twisted pair (**UTP**) and shielded twisted pair (**STP**).

Figure 5. A twisted pair wire.

Optical fiber is made of glass. It carries pulses of light that represent data (Figure 6). Some advantages of optical fiber over metal wires include its very low transmission loss and its immunity from electrical interference. Optical fibers can carry multiple wavelengths of light simultaneously. This greatly increases the data transmission rate — up to trillions of bits per second. Optical fibers can also support long runs of cable carrying very high data rates, so they are often used for undersea cables that connect continents.

Figure 6. Optical fibers.

Wireless Technologies

Forms of wireless technology include **terrestrial microwave** communication, which uses Earth-based transmitters and receivers that look like satellite dishes. Terrestrial microwaves are in the low-gigahertz frequency range, which limits transfer to devices that have clear line-of-sight between each other. Relay stations are spaced approximately 30 miles apart. **Free-space optical communication**, which uses visible or invisible light for communications, also requires line-of-sight in most cases, and this limits the physical positioning of communicating devices.

In contrast, **satellites** are a form of wireless technology stationed in space, typically in geosynchronous orbit 22,000 miles above the equator. These Earth-orbiting systems are capable of receiving and relaying voice, data, and TV signals. Satellites communicate via microwave radio waves, which are not deflected by the Earth's atmosphere. This means that normal weather does not generally affect the signal.

Cellular and **PCS systems** use several radio communication technologies. The systems divide the covered region into multiple geographic areas. Each area has a low-power transmitter or radio relay antenna device to relay calls from one area to the next. The towers typically seen in urban areas are transmitter and antenna arrays.

Wireless LANs use a high-frequency radio technology similar to digital cellular and an additional low-frequency radio technology (Figure 7). Wireless LANs also use **spread spectrum** technology to enable communication between multiple devices in a limited area. Wi-Fi is a common type of wireless radio-wave technology.

Network Nodes

Apart from any physical transmission medium, networks have basic system building blocks called nodes. These include network interface controllers, repeaters, hubs, bridges, switches, routers, modems, and firewalls.

A **network interface controller** (NIC) is hardware that enables a computer to access transmission media and to process low-level network information (Figure 8). For example, an NIC may have a connector for accepting a cable or an aerial receiver for wireless transmission and reception, as well as associated circuitry (Figure 9). The NIC responds to data transfers addressed to a network address for either the NIC or the computer as a whole.

In **Ethernet** networks, each network interface controller has a unique Media Access Control (MAC) address, usually stored in the NIC's permanent memory. To avoid address conflicts between network devices, the Institute of Electrical and Electronics Engineers (IEEE) maintains and administers MAC address uniqueness. The size of an Ethernet MAC address is six octets, each of which consists of eight digits of binary code. The three most significant octets are reserved to identify NIC manufacturers. These manufacturers, using their

Figure 7. A wireless network.

Figure 8. A NIC aerial reciever.

Figure 9. NIC aerial reciever.

assigned prefixes, uniquely assign the three least-significant octets of every Ethernet interface they produce.

A **repeater** is an electronic device that receives a network signal, clears unnecessary noise from the signal, and retransmits it. The signal is retransmitted at a higher

Figure 10. A network switch.

power level so that the signal can cover longer distances without degradation. Sometimes, a repeater receives a signal on one side of an obstruction that is blocking the signal and transmits it out on the other side. In most twisted-pair Ethernet configurations, repeaters are required for cable that runs longer than 100 meters. With fiber optics, repeaters can be tens or even hundreds of miles apart. A repeater with multiple ports is known as a **hub**.

A **network bridge** connects and filters traffic between two network segments to form a single network. Bridges come in three basic types — local, remote, and wireless. Local bridges directly connect LANs. Remote bridges can be used to create a WAN link between LANs. The connecting link may be slower than the end networks, so routers have mostly replaced this type of bridge. Wireless bridges join LANs or connect remote devices to LANs.

A **network switch** is a device that forwards and filters between ports based on the destination MAC address in each frame (Figure 10). A switch is distinct from a hub because it only forwards the frames to the physical ports involved in the communication rather than all ports connected. It can be thought of as a multi-port bridge.

Figure 11. A router.

A **router** is a networking device that forwards packets between networks by processing the routing information included in the packet. The routing information is often processed in conjunction with the routing or forwarding table. A router uses its routing table to determine where to forward packets (Figure 11).

Modems, or **modulator-demodulators,** are used to connect network nodes wirelessly or via wire that was not originally designed for digital network traffic, such as cable television or telephone wires. To do this, one or more carrier signals are modulated by the digital signal, producing an analog signal that can be tailored to the required properties for transmitting digital network traffic (Figure 12).

Figure 12. A modem.

A **firewall** is a network device for controlling network security and access rules. Firewalls are typically configured to reject access requests from unrecognized sources while allowing access from recognized sources. The vital role firewalls play in network security has grown with the increase of cyber-attacks (Figure 13).

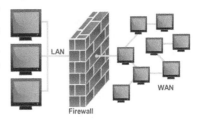

Figure 13. Diagram of a firewall.

2. Network Structure and Purpose

Network Structure

The structure of a network and the relationship between the nodes in that network make up what is known as the **network topology**, which determines the type and quality of functions that the network can perform (Figure 14).

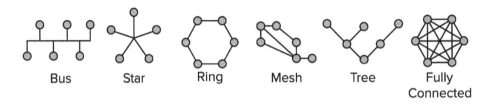

Figure 14. Different types of network topologies.

One of the most common topologies is a **bus topology**, which creates a network by connecting two or more hosts to a length of coaxial cabling. In this topology, a **terminator** must be placed on the end of the backbone coaxial cabling. This network is like a series of water pipes. If you can think of the data as water, the terminator is like a cap that prevents the water from flowing out of the network. This works well for smaller networks, such as one used by a small business that wants to securely transmit information between only a few computers in an office.

A **star topology** creates a network by arranging two or more host machines around a central hub. A variation of this topology, the star ring topology, is in common use today. A star topology is typically used in a broadcast network, where a single information source communicates directly with multiple clients. An example of this is a radio station, where a single antenna transmits data directly to many radios.

A **ring topology**, also known as a token ring topology, creates a network by arranging two or more hosts in a circle. Data are passed between hosts through a token. This token moves rapidly at all times throughout the ring, but in just one direction. If a host sends data to another host, it will attach those data to the token as it passes by, along with a piece of data saying who the message is for. The receiving host will see that the token has a message for it by scanning for destination MAC addresses that match its own. If the MAC addresses match, the receiving host will accept the data, and the message will be delivered. A ring topology makes a very stable network in which every networked device can both access the token and transmit through the token. Because a ring topology can handle a heavy network load more effectively than a bus topology, it is ideal for large organizations that need a network with both stability and security.

A **mesh topology** creates a network by ensuring that every host machine is connected to more than one other host machine on the local area network. In contrast to a bus topology, where the entire LAN will go down if one host fails, a mesh topology's main purpose is to prevent failure. In a mesh topology, as long as two machines with a working connection are still functioning, a LAN will still exist between them. Due to the reliability of a mesh topology and the opportunity for more than one path between a source and a destination, this type of topology is favored for wireless networks. However, it can be applied to wired networks as well.

With a **tree topology**, a root node forms the base of the network. The root node then communicates with a number of smaller nodes attached to it, and those in turn communicate with an even greater number of attached, smaller nodes. A host that branches off from the main tree is called a leaf. If a leaf fails, its connection is isolated and the rest of the LAN can continue onwards. A tree topology is basically a hybrid of a star topology and a bus topology, and can make it easy to expand an existing network. For this reason, it could be useful for a school that needs to increase the size of its network from time to time or for a growing company that needs to regularly expand.

An example of a tree topology network is the **Domain Name System** (DNS). DNS root servers connect to regional DNS servers. These connect to local DNS servers, which then connect with individual networks and individual computers. For your personal computer to talk to the root DNS server, it needs to send a request through the local DNS server, back through the regional DNS server, and then to the root server.

An **overlay network** is a network that is built on top of another network. Nodes in the overlay network are connected by virtual or logical links. Each of these corresponds to a path, perhaps through many physical links, in the underlying network.

A **fully connected network** is like an expanded mesh network. Every host is connected to every other host. While this may seem the best safeguard against failure, it is also costly to produce.

Organizational Scope

A network's organizational scope defines how the network is used — the number and type of users who are able to access it. Networks are typically managed by the organizations that own them. They may also provide network access to the Internet, which has no single owner and permits virtually unlimited global connectivity. Organizations can manage access to networks via intranets, extranets, internetworks, and the Internet.

An **intranet** is a network or set of networks under the control of a single administrator within an organization who restricts access to authorized users only. Most commonly, an intranet is the internal LAN of an organization, so the intranet uses IP protocols and IP-based tools such as web browsers and file transfer applications that members of the organization

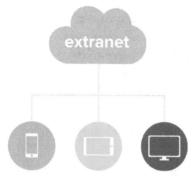

Figure 15. Diagram of an extranet.

need. A large intranet typically has at least one web server to provide users with organizational information. An intranet is also anything connected after the router in a LAN, even one you might have at home or at school.

An **extranet** is also under the administrative control of a single organization, but it supports a limited connection to a specific external network (Figure 15). For example, an organization may provide access to some aspects of its intranet in order to share data with its business partners or customers. These other entities are not necessarily trusted from a security standpoint, but are given extranet access to the intranet's content. These characteristics of an extranet make it useful for a manufacturer or merchandizer of physical products — one who needs to share internal information with suppliers, vendors, or customers but not with the wider world. Network connection to an extranet is often implemented via a WAN.

An **internetwork** is the connection of multiple computer networks via a common routing technology, using routers. The **Internet** is the largest example of an internetwork. It is a global system of interconnected government, academic, corporate, public, and private computer networks. It began as the Advanced Research Projects Agency Network (ARPANET), developed by the United States Department of Defense. The Internet is also the communications backbone underlying the World Wide Web (WWW).

Users connect to the Internet via a diverse array of methods, using several hundred documented and standardized Internet protocols compatible with the Internet Protocol Suite and an IP addressing system that is administered by the Internet Assigned Numbers Authority and by address registries.

Obviously, the Internet is vast, but estimates about its size have to account for different access levels in the Internet. These levels of access to data and available information are divided among the surface web, the deep web, and the darknet. For more information, see Chapter 7, "Internet Fundamentals."

Information Systems

Information systems are one of the most common ways that complementary networks are used to create, collect, organize, process, and distribute data within and between organizations. Organizations collect data on a large scale and use it to make decisions. Informing these decisions are predictions based on trends in the data and other analytics. This is called big data. Big data is the backbone of the information systems described in this section. Without the collection and analysis possible with big data, organizations' decision systems would be merely guesswork rather than research-based analyses.

Transaction processing is a style of computing that divides work into individual, indivisible operations, called transactions. A transaction processing system (TPS), or transaction server, is a combination of software and hardware that supports transaction processing. One common example of a transaction processing system would be the systems used by major credit card companies and found in almost every retail store (Figure 16).

A **management information system** (MIS) focuses on providing efficient tools to organize, evaluate, and manage departments for strategic decision-making within an organization. MIS professionals use these systems to help organizations get the most benefit from investments in personnel, equipment, and business processes.

A **decision support system** (DSS) is a computer-based information system that supports business or organizational decision-making activities. The management, operations, and planning levels of an organization use a DSS to help them make decisions about problems that may be rapidly changing and not easily identified in advance. A DSS is like a flow chart that sorts issues into categories through a series of questions or independent factors, and can be fully computerized, human-powered, or a combination of both. Three fundamental components of a DSS architecture are the database, the model, and the user interface.

A **database** is an organized collection of indexed data, usually stored as a group of linked data files that allow easy retrieval, updating, analysis, and output of information. These data can be stored in local files or distributed over a vast network of computers in the form of text, graphics, reports, scripts, tables, or text representing almost any kind of information (Figure 17). Many computer applications, including antivirus software, spreadsheets, and word-processors, are effectively databases.

Many databases today are built on a **relational database management system** (RDBMS). An RDBMS provides tools to design and develop tables, forms, queries, and reports. It is part of most modern commercial and open-source database systems, such as Oracle DB (Oracle Corporation), SQL Server (Microsoft), Access (Microsoft), MySQL (open source), Postgres (open source), and MariaDB (open source). These systems also have run-time subsystems that process queries, reports, and forms on request, turning the raw data into useful, readable information.

A **model-driven** DSS emphasizes access to and manipulation of a statistical, financial, optimization, or simulation model. Data and parameters provided by users assist decision-makers

Figure 16. Credit cards are processed by a TPS.

Figure 17. A database is a collection of data.

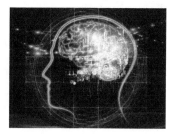

Figure 18. Artificial intelligence.

in analyzing a situation, but a model-driven DSS is not necessarily data-intensive. The model itself is more important. The model consists of the decision context and criteria the system uses, and the user interface is the way users interact with the system.

In artificial intelligence, an **expert system** is a computer system that emulates the decision-making ability of a human expert. Expert systems are designed to solve complex problems by reasoning. This process is represented primarily as if-then rules rather than conventional procedural code (Figure 18).

3. Communication Protocols, Routing, and Reliability

Communication Protocols

A communication protocol is a set of rules for exchanging network packets of information over network links. In a message sent digitally, all protocols join a "stack" where each protocol leverages the services of the protocol below it. An important example of a protocol stack is hypertext transfer protocol (**HTTP**, the World Wide Web protocol), which runs over transmission control protocol, and Internet protocol (**TCP/IP**), which runs over the Wi-Fi protocol (**IEEE 802.11**). This stack is used between the wireless router and the home user's personal computer when a user is surfing the web.

The complete **IEEE 802 protocol suite** provides a diverse set of networking capabilities. The protocols have a flat addressing scheme in which they operate mostly at the first and second levels of the protocol stack. **Ethernet** is sometimes simply called "LAN." It is a family of protocols used in wired LANs, described by a set of standards published by the IEEE that are together called IEEE 802.3. **Wireless LAN**, also widely known as WLAN or Wi-Fi, is probably the most well-known member of the IEEE 802 protocol family for home users today. It's standardized by IEEE 802.11 and shares many properties with wired Ethernet.

The **Internet protocol suite**, also called TCP/IP, is the foundation of all modern networking (Figure 19). It offers services over a network at the Internet protocol (IP) level. At its core, the protocol suite defines the addressing, identification, and routing specifications for **Internet Protocol version 4** (IPv4) and for **Internet Protocol version 6** (IPv6), the next generation of the protocol with enlarged addressing capabilities. For more information, see Chapter 7, "Internet Fundamentals."

Asynchronous transfer mode (ATM) is a switching technique for telecommunication networks. It uses asynchronous time-division multiplexing and encodes data into small, fixed-sized cells.

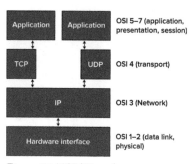

Figure 19. TCP/IP stack.

This differs from other protocols like the Internet protocol suite and Ethernet that use variable-sized packets or frames. ATM is similar to both circuit- and packet-switched networking, making it a good choice for a network that must handle both traditional high-throughput data traffic and real-time, low-latency content such as voice and video. ATM uses a connection-oriented model in which a virtual circuit must be established between two endpoints before the actual data exchange begins.

Synchronous optical networking (SONET) and **Synchronous Digital Hierarchy** (SDH) are standardized multiplexing protocols that use lasers to transfer multiple digital bit streams over optical fiber.

Routing

Routing is the process of selecting network paths to carry network traffic. Routing is performed for many kinds of networks, including circuit-switched networks and packet-switched networks.

In **packet-switched networks**, routing directs packet forwarding through intermediate network nodes. Intermediate nodes are typically network hardware devices such as routers, bridges, gateways, firewalls, or switches. General-purpose computers can also forward packets and perform routing, but because they are not specialized hardware, they will usually offer limited performance. As a result, most home computer networks use a router to direct traffic through the routing process more effectively. This process usually directs forwarding on the basis of **routing tables** that maintain a record of the routes to various network destinations. Constructing routing tables, which are held in the router's memory, is important for efficient routing.

There are usually multiple routes that traffic can take, and the router has to choose between them. A router stores and considers multiple types of information when deciding which routes are installed into the routing table, such as:

- Prefix length: longer subnet masks may be preferred, so this category of information may be relevant for a routing table

- Metric: if a lower metric/cost is preferred

- Administrative distance: when traffic is going between different routing protocols, a lower distance may be preferred

Most routing tables use algorithms to make these decisions, and they use only one network path at a time. However, there are also multipath routing techniques that enable the use of many alternative paths.

Bridging is still widely used within local environments, but routing has become the dominant form of addressing on the Internet. Routing is often contrasted with bridging in its assumption that network addresses are structured and that similar addresses imply proximity within the network. Structured addresses allow a single routing table entry to represent the one best route to a group of devices. In large networks, the structured addressing of routing has better performance than unstructured addressing of bridging.

Reliability and Security

There are many ways to measure the performance of a network because each network is different in design. Performance can also be modeled instead of measured. **Quality of service** (QoS) is the ability to provide different priority to different applications, users, or data flows or to guarantee a certain level of performance to a data flow. The parameters that affect QoS typically can include throughput, jitter, bit error rate, and latency.

Network performance can also be measured by network congestion and network resilience. **Network congestion** occurs when a link or node is carrying so much data that its quality of service deteriorates. Typical effects include queuing delay, packet loss, or blocking of new connections. A consequence of these latter two is that incremental increases in offered load lead to either a small increase in network throughput or an actual reduction in network throughput.

Network resilience measures the network's ability to maintain quality of service. To increase the resilience of a network, administrators must identify the probable challenges and risks within the network and define appropriate resilience metrics for the service to be protected from those risks.

Computer security, also known as cyber security or IT security, involves protecting information systems from theft or damage to their hardware, software, and information, as well as from any disruption or misdirection of the services they provide.

Network security consists of policies adopted by the network administrator to prevent and monitor unauthorized access, misuse, modification, or denial of the computer network and its network-accessible resources. Network security is covered further in Chapter 8, "Security and Safety."

Network surveillance is the monitoring of data transferred over computer networks such as the Internet. The monitoring is often secret and may be done either directly or ordered by governments, corporations, criminal organizations, or individuals. Surveillance may be legal or illegal. Legal surveillance may require authorization from a court or other independent agency.

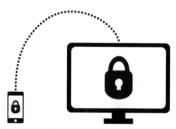

Figure 20. End-to-end encryption.

End-to-end encryption (E2EE) is a digital communications paradigm covering uninterrupted protection of data traveling between two communicating hosts (Figure 20). In E2EE, the sender encrypts data so only the intended receiver can decrypt them, with no dependence on other parties. E2EE prevents intermediaries, such as Internet providers or application service providers, from discovering or tampering with communications. End-to-end encryption generally protects both confidentiality and integrity.

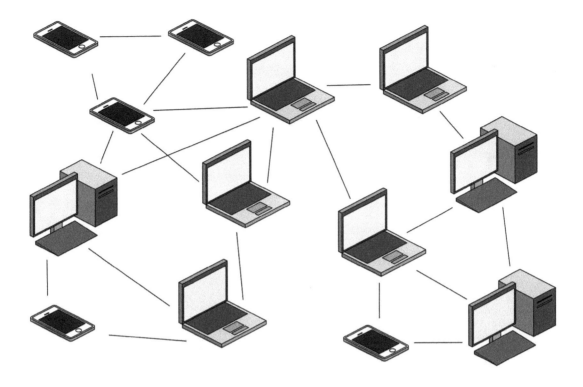

Figure 21. There are many network services available.

Chapter 6
Electronic Communication

When you use computers to communicate with others, you consider things like how long the message is, whether it's private or public, and what the format of that message is. This chapter looks closely at three important ways that computers can be used to communicate — email, real-time communication, and social media. It will also explore the best ways to use those communication tools and the etiquette — or "netiquette" — for online communication, which is an increasingly important issue as more and more of our communication is done digitally.

1. Email

Electronic mail, or **email**, is a digital message that is sent from one author to one or more recipients via the Internet or other computer networks. Users can create, send, and receive messages using an email application on their computers or an online, browser-based application.

Early email systems were like instant messaging because the author and recipient of a message had to be online at the same time. Today's email systems are based on a store-and-forward model. Email messages are stored on servers that send, accept, and forward messages automatically. Users need to briefly connect to those servers for the client to send or receive messages, but the sender and receiver do not have to be connected simultaneously.

Email messages consist of a message header and a message body. The message header contains control information, which at a minimum includes the sender's email address and one or more recipient addresses. The header can also include more descriptive information, such as a subject line or title for a message, and a date and time stamp that records when the message was submitted to the server. Other information, such as "In-reply-to" information that causes later messages in that thread to be marked with "RE:" or carbon copy (CC) or blind carbon copy (BCC), is also located in headers. The main text of the message is called the message body. Senders also have the option to attach files to a message which the receivers can then download from the message.

The **Post Office Protocol 3** (POP3) is a set of mail access protocols used by a client application to read messages from a connected mail server. POP3 supports simple download-and-delete requirements for access to remote mailboxes, so messages received by the client are frequently deleted from the server.

Figure 1.

The **Internet Message Access Protocol** (IMAP) lets users manage a mailbox from multiple devices. This is useful for Internet users who use small portable devices like smartphones to check email while travelling or to make brief replies on the go. IMAP displays the headers, the sender, and the subject. Usually, messages are stored in folders in the mail server until the device makes a request to download a specific message.

Many email providers offer a **web-based** email client such as Gmail, Outlook, and Yahoo! Mail. This allows users to log into their email account in any compatible web browser to send and receive their email. Messages are not typically downloaded to the client, so these can't be read without a current Internet connection.

Mobile apps for email mean that accessibility is now constant, even when users are away from home or work. Alerts can be sent to the phone to notify users of new messages as soon as these are received. As a result, email is used more frequently to communicate as users check their email and write messages throughout the day. Today, an estimated 1.4 billion people use email worldwide, and send an average of 50 billion non-spam emails every day.

For casual use, email provides almost instant communication across great distances, making it easier than ever to maintain friendships and other relationships via written messages. It's also the most widely used medium for business communication. A 2010 study on workplace communication by Paytronics found that 83% of U.S. knowledge workers — whose work exists primarily in a digital form — considered email to be critical to their success and productivity at work.

One of the most common sources of business-related email is email **marketing**, which has grown significantly via "opt-in" agreements. These agreements allow businesses to connect directly with individual customers, making targeted marketing more efficient. Email is often used to send special sales offers and new product information to customers who have opted in to receiving email from that business. This is more effective than unsolicited email to users who have not. Hyperlinks or generic information on consumer trends are less effective since email sent without permission from users — they have not "opted in" — is likely to be viewed as unwelcome or identified as **spam**, which is defined further below.

Problems with Email

The usefulness of email is frequently threatened by several common problems.

Flaming is sending email that contains angry or antagonizing content. Flaming is likely more common today because of how easy it is to send an impersonal email. Confrontations in person or via telephone require more direct interaction. Social norms encourage civility, so people tend to be less likely to lash out in these communications. By comparison, typing a message to another person is an indirect interaction, so the expected civility can be more easily forgotten.

Email messages may have one or more attachments that deliver files along with messages, and sometimes those attachments become a problem. There's no technical restriction in the protocol governing email that limits the size or number of attachments. In practice, however, email service providers implement their own limitations on the allowed size of individual files or the size of an entire message. Attachments that violate those limitations will keep users from sending large files via their otherwise convenient email system.

Email bankruptcy occurs when a user ignores a large number of email messages after he or she falls behind in reading and answering them. Frequent users of email can fall behind because of information overload, a general sense there is so much information that it is not possible to read it all. It's not hard to imagine this happening when we think about 50 billion messages sent every day to only 1.4 billion users. That's nearly 50 messages per person!

Any unwanted message is called **spam**, but spam takes many forms, and may often contribute to the email bankruptcy mentioned above. Email spamming means actively sending unwanted email to recipients (Figure 2). For example, if you donate to political parties or candidates, they may send you more and more frequent reminders to donate again. What was once an intentional gift on your part may quickly turn into increased spam messages asking for more.

Email bombing is intentionally sending large volumes of messages to a target address. Overloading the target email address with thousands of messages at once can render it unusable and can even cause the mail server to crash (Figure 3).

Email phishing is when senders try to trick recipients into sending them sensitive information. A phishing email is spam that contains a subject header or message body that makes the message appear as if it came from a known or trusted source. Phishing email tries to gain information like passwords to otherwise secured accounts by providing links to false or "spoof" websites that have been carefully designed to look like the real thing. Entering your online shopping login and password on a spoof website might result in your shopping account being charged for purchases made by a phishing sender who now has your login information. Although not all phishing emails have dangerous content like viruses or malware, many contain links to websites that, if you're not careful, could result in your information being shared with others (Figure 4).

Most email applications have quick ways to filter out and report suspicious email messages such as phishing, but the sophistication and careful design of phishing messages seems to always be increasing. Since phishers don't necessarily have your real name but your online

Figure 2. A botnet operator will sell access to their bot to spammers.

Figure 3. Email bombing is sending large volumes of messages.

Figure 4. Phishing tries to trick people into sending sensitive information.

accounts usually do, one way to identify a possible phishing message is to see if your name is not mentioned in the message body. Retail websites like eBay and Amazon have special sections advising users about how to avoid phishing schemes.

Many users, both casual and professional, have concerns about the **email privacy**. Email may seem instantaneous, but the reality is that it takes time to travel between sender and recipient. During the transit time, it's possible for third parties to read or even modify the content.

Figure 5. Email has potential privacy concerns.

At this point, the differences between Internet and internal email systems become more relevant. Internet email may travel and be stored on networks and computers without the sender's or the recipient's control, while internal mail systems send information that never leaves the closed organizational network. Internal mail systems sound more secure than Internet systems, but information technology personnel who monitor or manage communications have the potential to violate the privacy of other employees by accessing their email.

Potential problems with email don't stop there. Email does not typically use any kind of encryption, making it possible for someone with your account login information to read or even send emails from your account. Many ISPs store copies of email messages on their mail servers before the messages are delivered. The backups of these messages can remain on the server for up to several months, despite users deleting them from their mailboxes. Additionally, many mail user agents do not protect logins and passwords, making them easy to intercept by an attacker.

We discuss methods to ensure better security for your personal information and data in Chapter 8, "Security and Safety."

2. Real-Time Communication

Web Real-Time Communication

Web Real-Time Communication (WebRTC) supports browser-to-browser applications for voice calling, video chat, and peer-to-peer (P2P) file sharing without needing any kind of plugins. WebRTC is a work in progress based on other preliminary projects with similar goals, such as P2P data transfers and other real-time communication.

The major components of WebRTC include sets of scripts that developers can use to create applications and their features. Some of the most important scripts are getUserMedia, which allows a web browser to access a device's camera and microphone and to capture media; RTCPeerConnection, which sets up audio and video calls; RTCDataChannel, which allows browsers to share data via P2P; and getStats, which allows the web application to retrieve a set of statistics about WebRTC sessions. These standards were developed by the WebRTC working group at the World Wide Web Consortium, a group that defines and publishes standards for web development.

By deploying a WebRTC gateway, users are able to access the Session Initiation Protocol (SIP)-based private branch exchange (PBX) telephone systems and call centers. WebRTC hosts the existing PBX system, which allows multiple phone users to call locally within a large organization and switch between a limited number of external lines — without the need to change these services. Incoming calls to the organization are handled by a WebRTC gateway of the service provider. Incoming WebRTC calls are translated into SIP calls and routed to the organization. The organization does not have to change anything in its infrastructure because it will still be only handling SIP calls.

WebRTC has the potential to meet the needs of both individual and business users in a variety of ways. When finished, WebRTC will be supported without the need for additional applications or browser plug-ins, making it accessible to any users with a supported browser. WebRTC also enhances communication with rich content, including video, without the need for special applications and servers.

Private users will have access to a wider range of communication methods and add-ons through the use of apps instead of additional hardware. They will be able to make voice calls without having to plug in a telephone — or receive a phone bill. For businesses, WebRTC will be embedded into web pages so customers don't have to leave their current page to start a voice and video call with the customer service department. This saves money by replacing the toll-free telephone numbers for call centers.

WebRTC also requires encryption for both the media and the electronic signaling between communicators, so another benefit is a higher security level than most currently-available commercial telephony systems. This is particularly useful for businesses who can secure communications with their customers, as well as employees in home offices or remote branches.

Telepresence

Telepresence refers to a set of technologies that allow people to look or feel as if they are present somewhere other than their actual physical location. Visual and sound information travels in both directions between a local user and others in a remote location, just as it would between participants in a face-to-face conversation. With videoconferencing, for example, users in remote locations share visual and sound information in order to simulate the sort of discussion that would happen if they were all in the same location (Figure 6).

Figure 6. Telepresence can help business bring remote workers together virtually.

At a minimum, a telepresence system must include visual

feedback. For a more immersive experience, the user's entire field of view should be filled with a view of the remote location, and the remote user's viewpoint should correspond to the movement and orientation of the local user's display. In this way, telepresence differs from television or cinema, in which the viewpoint is not controlled by the viewer.

Video telepresence requires greater technical sophistication and greater fidelity of both sight and sound than traditional videoconferencing. Technical advancements in mobile collaboration have also extended the capabilities of videoconferencing to hand-held mobile devices, enabling collaboration without the need to be in a conference room or some other technology hub.

A more advanced telepresence example is in the field of robotics. Where remote manipulation of robotic equipment is possible, the ability to manipulate a remote object or environment can be implemented in number of ways. Typically, the movements of the user's hands are sensed by wired gloves, inertia sensors, or absolute spatial position sensors. A robot in the remote location then copies those movements as closely as possible. This process is also

known as teleoperation. Haptic teleoperation refers to a system that provides some sort of tactile force feedback to the user, so the user feels some approximation of the weight, firmness, size, or texture of the remote objects manipulated by the robot. The complexity of usable robotics varies greatly, from simple, one-axis grippers to lifelike robotic hands. The more closely the robot recreates the actions of the human hand, the greater the sense of telepresence (Figure 7).

The increased availability of high-quality video conferencing tools via mobile devices, tablets, and other portable computers has caused a drastic growth in telepresence robots (Figure 8). Drivable versions typically contain a display, which is usually a phone or tablet mounted on a roaming base. Some examples of roaming telepresence robots include Beam by Suitable Technologies, Double by Double Robotics, RP-Vita by iRobot, Anybots, Vgo, TeleMe by Mantarobot, and Romo by Romotive Live Presence Robot. More modern roaming telepresence robots may include an ability to operate autonomously. The robots could scan and map out the space and be able to avoid obstacles while driving themselves between rooms and their docking stations.

Figure 7. Robots can be used for teleoperations.

Figure 8. A telepresence robot.

Telepresence's effectiveness is usually related to its quality or fidelity, from high-quality "immersive" fidelity, to mid-range "adaptive," and finally, "lite" solutions. Immersive solutions are highly controlled at both ends of the connection with respect to lighting, acoustics, décor, and furniture, giving all the participants the impression they are together in the same room, hence the "immersive" label. Adaptive telepresence solutions may use this same technology, but the environments at both ends are not highly controlled, removing the sense that all the participants are in the same space. Adaptive solutions differ from lite solutions not in terms of environment control but in terms of technology integration. Adaptive solutions use a managed service, while lite solutions use components that someone must integrate, like an add-on instead of a native feature.

Telepresence communication offers many benefits to its users. Rather than traveling great distances for face-to-face meetings, for example, it's now common to use a telepresence system to simulate that meeting. Participants use a telepresence room to dial in to the meeting, so they can see and talk with the other participants as if they were in the same room. This brings enormous benefits compared to other collaborative technology like email threads or even phone conferencing. The visual aspect greatly enhances communication, allowing for perception of facial expressions and other body language. Mobile collaboration systems combine the use of video, audio, and on-screen drawing capabilities using hand-held mobile devices.

Figure 9. The Mars Exploration Rovers are teleoperated from Earth.

Beyond business, applications of telepresence can be found in emergency and hazard management, industrial inspection, health, and education. Small-diameter pipes otherwise inaccessible for examination can now be viewed using pipeline video inspection. Hazardous environments like mining, bomb disposal, military operations, rescue of victims from fire, toxic atmospheres, deep sea exploration, or even hostage situations are good candidates for telepresence applications so that humans can stay at a safer distance from those hazards. Telepresence also plays a critical role in technology used for exploring other worlds, such as the Mars Exploration Rovers, which are teleoperated from Earth (Figure 9).

Figure 10. A surgeon performing a teleoperation.

The knowledge and physical skill of surgeons are in such consistently high demand that transmitting their knowledge and skill rather than transporting patients or surgeons is a very attractive possibility. There is considerable current research in this direction. Locally controlled robots are being used for joint replacement surgeries because they are more precise in milling bone to receive new joints (Figure 10). The military also has an obvious interest in this medical application. The combination of telepresence, teleoperation, and telerobotics could mean potentially saving lives in battle with quick access to surgeons operating from outside combat zones.

The application of telepresence also shows promise in education. The JASON and NASA Ames Research Center programs explore the benefits of using telepresence to let students take an active part in exploration. Students or researchers can explore an otherwise inaccessible location using robotic telepresence. Sites where the passage of too many people is harming the immediate environment or the artifacts themselves — undersea coral reefs, ancient Egyptian tombs, and precious works of art — can become accessible using these technologies.

Remote classrooms allow a single professor to interact with students in multiple campuses simultaneously. The law schools of Rutgers University currently use this application. Two identical rooms, located in two metropolitan areas, are equipped with studio lighting, audio, and video conference equipment connected to a 200-inch monitor on the wall that students face, giving the impression of being all in the same classroom. This allows professors to be on either campus and facilitates the interaction among students at both campuses during the classes.

3. Social Media

Social media may seem synonymous with electronic communication these days, but they are a relatively new advancement. Social media are services and applications that provide tools for people or companies to create, share, or exchange information. This information could be career interests, ideas, pictures, videos, or nearly anything else. These applications depend on mobile and web-based technologies to create highly interactive platforms through which individuals and communities share, co-create, discuss, and modify the user-generated content. These new types of media have caused widespread, significant changes in the way people interact with one another.

With the variety of specialized social media platforms, the uses for social media are very broad. According to 2011 Pew Research data, nearly 80% of American adults are online and nearly 60% of them use social networking sites. The following data from a Pew Internet Research Survey in 2011 show how many Internet users create different kinds of content:

- 65 percent of Internet users write material on a social media site such as Facebook or Twitter.
- 55 percent share photos.
- 37 percent contribute rankings and reviews of products or services.
- 33 percent create tags for linking content.
- 26 percent post comments on third-party websites or blogs.
- 15 percent take online material and remix it into a new creation with photos, video, audio, or text.
- 14 percent have created or work on a blog.

In a 2016 follow-up study, Pew Research found that social media have become an integral part of the lives of even more people:

- 79% of all adult Internet users use Facebook, 76% of whom use it every day.
- 32% use Instagram, 51% of whom use it every day.

- 24% use Twitter, 42% of whom use it every day.

One of social media content's distinguishing components is its **virality** — the greater like-lihood that users will share content posted by others in their network. Many social media sites provide specific functionality to help users easily and quickly re-share content, such as Twitter's retweet button, Pinterest's pin, or Tumblr's reblog function.

Businesses have a particular interest in virality for marketing purposes. When content "goes viral," it spreads information quickly across a vast number of platforms and user networks. Corporations attempt to create viral content to spread information about their products, while nonprofit organizations and activists may have similar interests in viral content supporting their causes.

While browser-based social media offer a variety of opportunities for companies in many different business sectors, mobile social media make use of the location and time-sensitive aspects of individual users' lives. Mobile social-media applications such as Pinterest — where users post links to retail items or blogs and sort them with "pins" like they would on a virtual bulletin board — have contributed to greater popularity and accessibility of online purchasing. The potential for businesses' social media use is particularly valuable in marketing research, sales promotions, discounts, and relationship developments like loyalty programs. Mobile social-media applications offer data about consumers' physical movements in more detail than ever before. A company can now know the exact time a customer entered one of its outlets, as well as any comments made during the visit.

Encouraging social media use as part of a consumer experience is a way to integrate shopping with entertaining activities and a way for marketing researchers to extract relatively intrusive data about their customer bases without seeming intrusive at all. When stores hang a sign encouraging users to tweet or post online with a specific "hashtag" — a sorting tag that links messages together based on common use of the tag — they are asking you to voluntarily join in the broad collection of shopping data (Figure 11).

Although in the past customers had to use printed coupons from traditional print media, mobile social media now allow companies to tailor sales promotions and discounts to specific users at specific times by sending them links to sales promotions through social media. In order to increase long-term relationships with customers, companies can construct loyalty programs that allow customers who check in or post regularly at a company's locations to earn discounts or other perks like free services or products.

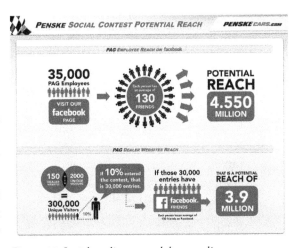

Figure 11. Social media can reach large audiences.

Differences Between Social and Industrial Media

The growth of social media has occurred in stages over the past twenty years (2). More Americans get their news via the Internet than from newspapers or radio, and three-fourths of Americans say they get news from updates via email or social media sites, according to a report published by CNN in 2010[1]. The survey suggests that Facebook and Twitter make news a more participatory experience than before as people share news articles and comment on others' posts. 75% of people get their news forwarded through email or social media posts, and 37% of people shared a news item via Facebook or Twitter. Prior to the rise of social media, however, people in industrialized countries traditionally obtained information, education, news, and other data from industrial media such as print and television.

The process of creating industrial media requires significant resources. With print, for example, there is the obvious cost of ink and paper and printing presses, but behind that are the costs that go into creating and revising publications before printing. Other industrial media like television and film require even greater resources for equipment, studios, and specialized personnel. Social media, on the other hand, are comparably inexpensive to create and publish. Most social media production only requires a reuse of existing skills rather than specialized skills. Anyone — even private individuals — can produce material quickly and cheaply. Because the quality of our electronic devices for image and video capture has improved so much in recent years, it's even affordable to produce video content without the need for expensive equipment or studios.

The time between ideas and production in industrial media can be weeks, months, or even years. Industrial media, once created, can't easily be altered, either. For example, once a magazine article is printed and distributed, changes cannot be made to that same article until later print runs. Social media, on the other hand, can be created and published almost instantaneously. If changes need to be made, those are also instantaneous.

Both industrial and social media are capable of reaching a global audience. Industrial media typically use a centralized framework for organization, production, and distribution. This system means that the publishers have direct control over the quality of content and use that control to produce higher quality products that will be more valuable to users. They're less likely to release low-quality content because that won't generate the sales they need to pay for the publishing framework. Social media are necessarily decentralized, with little organization beyond individual networks. Social media tools are generally available to the public at little or no cost. Anyone can publish anything, in other words. One main challenge posed by content in social media is that the quality varies so widely because it's published without the quality control of industrial media.

---

[1]Doug Gross, "Survey: More Americans Get News from Internet than Newspapers or Radio," CNN.com, March 1, 2010, http://www.cnn.com/2010/TECH/03/01/social.network.news/index.html.

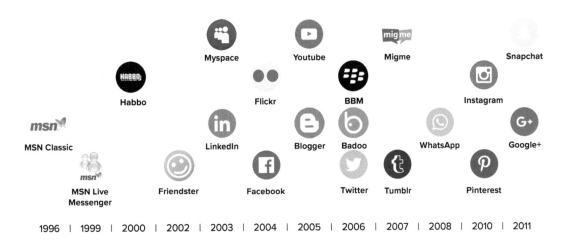

Figure 12. Chart showing a timeline of social media.

One characteristic shared by both media is the uncertainty over whether something will reach a large audience or a small one. For example, a single blog post or television show has the potential to reach zero people or millions of people, depending on the circumstances. Today it seems like anything can go viral and reach a large audience, but at the same time, any television show or film or book or blog posting might also find itself without any audience.

Social media have provided an open arena where people are free to exchange ideas on companies, brands, and products. Social media provide an environment where users and marketing professionals can interact, and where advertisers can promote their brand and improve their company's image by listening and responding to what the public is saying about their product. Focus groups have been a staple of market research for decades, but now these groups can happen more quickly, with less planning, and without necessarily having to compensate responders if volunteers are willing to participate. Social media can positively affect social standing and help activists and candidates gain political support (Figure 13).

Figure 13. Benefits of social media.

Problems with Social Media

As social networking becomes more popular across all generations, sites such as Facebook and YouTube have gradually undermined the traditionally authoritative voices of news media. Because traditional media have historically shaped the collective memories of past important events, the loss of that shaping control is seen as a danger by some media scholars and leaders.

Figure 14. Privacy is always a concern on social media.

Because large-scale collaborative co-creation is one of the main ways of forming information in a social network, unedited user-generated content has to be viewed with skepticism by readers.

In his 2008 article, "Is Google Making Us Stupid?"[2], Nicholas Carr notes that "fast (social) media and deep slow thought don't mix well." Carr cites other writers and readers who suffer from a loss of concentration when trying to read more than a few pages at a time. The "power-browsing" of modern Internet use — where users skip from one thing to the next, mixing work with entertainment and social media interactions — has caused a shift in the way our brains function to process information. When all we get from our media is a series of sound-bite-sized pieces of information, anything longer than a sound bite causes us to lose focus and feels like a chore.

Privacy-rights advocates also warn users about the information being gathered through social media (Figure 14). Some information is captured without the user's knowledge or consent, through methods such as electronic tracking and third-party applications on social networks. Other risks include law enforcement and governmental use of this information, including the gathering of so-called social media intelligence through data mining techniques.

Finally, the "digital divide" refers to economic disparity and the resulting impact on access to technology (Figure 15). The disparity exists between people of different socioeconomic levels or other demographic categories (Figure 16). Some scholars claim that within our modern information society, some individuals produce Internet content while others only consume it, which could be a result of disparities in the education system where only some teachers integrate technology into the classroom and teach critical thinking. While there are differences among age groups in use of social media, a 2010 study in the United States found no racial divide.

Figure 15. Relatively few countries have the same widespread technological use as the US.

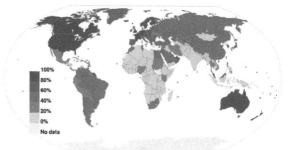

Figure 16. Global percentage of population's internet access.

[2]Nicholas Carr, "Is Google Making Us Stupid," Atlantic Monthly, July/August 2008, http://www.theatlantic.com/magazine/archive/2008/07/is-google-making-us-stupid/306868/.

4. Technology Etiquette

"Etiquette" is a word used to describe the rules of behavior and manners in social situations. In our daily lives, we practice good etiquette when we avoid interrupting someone who is speaking, we hold the door for someone who has their hands full, or we politely ask for directions. Social interactions are much easier and friendlier when etiquette is considered.

The rules of etiquette when communicating over the Internet are different from those that apply when communicating in person or by telephone. Online communications are prone to misunderstandings because they lack facial expressions and body language to help audiences interpret the meaning of the text. Because of the anonymity that online communication affords, these communications are also open to abuse. People are more willing to be rude or offensive when they don't feel that they will be held accountable for their words.

Etiquette in computer-based communication — also known as "**netiquette**" — refers to behavior that is socially acceptable in an online or digital situation. Others refer to good online manners as **digital citizenship**, a broader term that describes how a person should act while using digital technology online. The term is often mentioned in relation to Internet safety and netiquette, but it also covers communication via mobile devices, such as texting (Figure 17).

Figure 17. As with any communication, there are rules of etiquette.

Because most Internet communication still happens as text, the descriptions of netiquette below mostly apply to text communication. Part of netiquette involves recommendations for avoiding misunderstandings or causing emotions to flare into a heated discussion in the first place. In addition, netiquette provides rules against disrupting the ease of reading online communication, such as adding distracting or misleading posts.

Here are some key guidelines for netiquette:

1. Respect the privacy of others. Sharing information can be done so easily now that respecting privacy may not seem as obvious as it would in face-to-face interactions. Respecting privacy online ranges from not sharing personal data to not forwarding a private message. Some users take the privacy of their posts for granted, particularly in more private communications like email. But privacy isn't automatic because text messages can be captured with a screenshot and shared with anyone. Before you broadcast someone's private post across the Internet, ask permission. Remember that your own posts can easily be made public, too.

2. Avoid multi-posting and cross-posting. If you post the same message or content more than once, that's **multi-posting**. Whether you do so on purpose or by mistake, this repetitiveness is obnoxious at best, and disrespectful to the original posters at worst. **Cross-posting** is submitting or sending the same message to multiple different threads. Cross-posting a question can be advantageous to the poster because it increases the number of answers received, but for recipients, it can get repetitive and annoying (Figure 18).

3. Avoid off-topic posting. In the context of mailing lists, discussion groups, discussion forums, bulletin boards, newsgroups, and wikis, a post is off-topic if it is *not* within the bounds of the current discussion. Even on very specialized forums and lists, off-topic posting is not necessarily frowned upon, but a common netiquette convention is to mark a new off-topic posting or email by beginning it with "OT." For example, in a forum discussing the Linux operating system, someone might post: "OT: Wow, did you feel that earthquake?" Repeated or targeted off-topic posting might be seen as "hijacking" a thread, which turns a conversation on one topic toward an entirely new topic. This makes the title of the thread meaningless because it no longer aligns with the thread's content. This in turn wastes the time of users who come to a thread thinking they'll find one thing, only to be surprised by all the off-topic posting.

4. Keep your electronic signature simple. An electronic signature is a block of text automatically added at the bottom of an email or thread message. For business purposes, keep it plain and simple to avoid confusing readers. Your signature block should contain, at minimum, your name, title, and organization. More than that should only be included if necessary, such as a contact phone number or address (Figure 19). Elsewhere on the Internet, signature blocks have been known to include digital art and pictures or a pithy quote that the user wants to share. In those contexts, make sure that your signature fits in with those from other users.

5. Don't use all caps. Avoid typing in all capital letters or grossly enlarging script for emphasis. This is considered equivalent to yelling. It wouldn't be socially acceptable to yell at someone in person, so don't yell at them online.

6. Help readers interpret your words. Perhaps the biggest obstacle to communication in online settings is the lack of nonverbal cues to help your audience know how to take something you have written. Facial cues can dictate the mood and corresponding word choice of two people in a face-to-face conversation. During phone conversations, tone of voice communicates

Figure 18. Posting the same thing on multiple platforms is cross-posting.

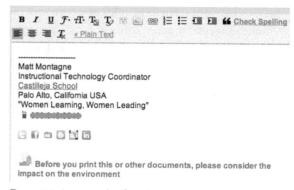

Figure 19. An example of an electronic signature.

the emotions of the person on the other line, although not as well as face-to-face conversation. But with online communication, any signals that would indicate people's emotional states or the tone of their words are unavailable. In recent years, there have been some interesting developments to try to accommodate this.

Figure 20. A Smiley face emoticon.

Emoticons use punctuation marks combined visually to illustrate common iconic facial expressions (Figure 20). For example, a colon and an end parenthesis creates the symbol of a smiling face. This could indicate the happiness or satisfaction of the person who sent the emoticon. **Abbreviations** also achieve some emotional context. To symbolize laughter, users can also send the abbreviation "LOL," which stands for "laughing out loud." Countless other symbols and abbreviations have developed, including "BRB" ("be right back") and "TTYL" ("talk to you later"). Small graphic designs called **emoji** incorporate a huge range of pictorial symbols from a laughing face, sad face, crying face, and angry face to symbols for animals, activities, and objects (Figure 21). Since their first appearance on Japanese mobile phones in the 1990s, emoji have experienced an explosion of worldwide popularity. Apple has included them on its iPhone, followed by Android and other mobile operating systems.

Figure 21. Emoji examples.

7. **Pay attention to and follow developing rules of etiquette.** As new modes of communication become more common, the rules of communication etiquette will adapt as quickly as the technology. The popular app Snapchat, for example, allows users send pictures or videos that disappear a few seconds after being viewed. The reply option has turned the app into a popular tool for sending pictures back and forth. Most users now agree that a snap that has been personalized for the receiver should expect a reply. That's a new expectation — a new rule of etiquette — for this new app. Hundreds of new apps appear each year, and over time each will develop its own set of expectations for your behavior. For you to use those apps to communicate successfully, you'll need to pay attention to those new rules and follow them.

Chapter 7
Internet Fundamentals

The Internet is a network of networks. It is a global system of interconnected mainframe, personal, and wireless computer networks that use the Internet protocol suite (TCP/IP) to link billions of devices worldwide. Within the Internet, there are millions of participating networks that are all linked together by a broad array of electronic, wireless, and optical networking technologies.

This chapter will look first at the elements and history of the Internet as a whole. Then it will focus on the most popular and noticeable part of the Internet, the World Wide Web, and the web browser applications that allow you to use that part of the Internet.

Figure 1.

1. The Internet

The origins of the Internet date back to research and development commissioned by governments in the United States, the United Kingdom, and France in the 1960s. The goal was to build robust, fault-tolerant communication between computer networks.

In the United States, these efforts led to the development of the Advanced Research Projects Agency Network (**ARPANET**), the main foundation for what would become the Internet. ARPANET was initially funded by the Advanced Research Projects Agency (ARPA) of the United States Department of Defense (Figure 2). This network pioneered the packet-switching and TCP/IP technologies that became the technical foundation for the Internet. ARPANET transmitted its first message in 1968. In 1970, ARPANET reached the East Coast of the United States (Figure 4). By 1981 there were 213 host computers, with a new host connecting approximately every twenty days.

Figure 2. United States Department of Defense Emblem.

In 1982, the **Internet Protocol Suite** (TCP/IP) was standardized. TCP/IP is the set of rules that computers follow when they send data packets to and from each other on the Internet. This development allowed interconnected networks access to ARPANET from anywhere in the world. The standardizing of these rules also enabled the rise of the commercial Internet service providers (ISPs) that began to emerge in the late 1980s and early 1990s. The ARPANET was decommissioned in 1990.

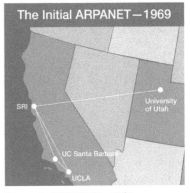

Figure 3. ARPNET in 1969.

Packet switching — now the dominant basis for data communications worldwide — was a new concept at the dawn of the ARPANET. Packet switching is accomplished by collecting data into groups, rather than sending data as an individual stream of bits, and then transmitting these groups, or packets, onto the attached network link as soon as the link becomes available. The link can be used to send multiple packets to different destination stations, much like a post office mailbox can be used to post letters to different destinations. For Internet traffic, this is more effective than the circuit-switching model it replaced, which worked like a telephone call in the sense that an individual sender sends an individual and continuous message to an individual receiver.

Hypertext Transfer Protocol (HTTP) is an application protocol for distributed, collaborative, hypermedia information systems (Figure 4). HTTP is the protocol used to successfully exchange or transfer hypertext, and is the foundation of data communication on the World Wide Web. The HTTP protocol has been expanded to include a separate protocol for secured connections, called HTTPS. The "S" indicates a secure connection.

Hypertext is structured text that uses logical links — hyperlinks — between nodes containing text. HTTP functions as a request-response request protocol in a client-server model. A web browser, for example, may be the client and an application running on a different computer hosting a website may be the server. The client submits an HTTP request message to the server. The server, which provides resources such as files and other content or performs other functions on behalf of the client, then returns a response message to the client. The response contains status information about the request, and may also contain requested content in its message body.

Figure 4. HTTP allows for communication on the World Wide Web.

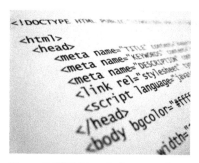

Figure 5. HTML is the language for creating websites.

HyperText Markup Language (HTML) is the standard markup language used to create web pages (Figure 5). Along with CSS and JavaScript, HTML is a cornerstone technology of web pages and user interfaces for mobile and web applications. Web browsers "read" the HTML files and render them into visible and/or audible web pages. HTML describes the structure of a website along with cues for presentation, which makes it a markup language rather than a programming language.

All these ingredients — the networks, languages, protocols, and users — make the Internet possible. The vastness of the Internet today was only a dream just a few decades ago, and no one knows how big it will become, or how it may change in the near future.

Governance

Efforts to standardize and maintain the Internet are an important part of its continuing usefulness. The type of government and educational leaders who have traditionally guided the development of the Internet have been joined by programming experts to help define the Internet's limits and its capability moving forward. Though the Internet has no central governing body, several organizations work together to keep the Internet running. These organizations are mainly responsible for forming protocols and standards that Internet developers must follow for their work to function on the World Wide Web.

The technical underpinning and standardization of the core protocols (IPv4 and IPv6) is an activity of the Internet Engineering Task Force (IETF), a nonprofit organization of loosely affiliated international participants that anyone may associate with by contributing technical expertise.

To maintain interoperability, the principal name spaces of the Internet are administered by the Internet Corporation for Assigned Names and Numbers (ICANN). ICANN is governed by an international board of directors drawn from across the Internet's technical, business, academic, and noncommercial communities (Figure 6). ICANN coordinates the assignment of unique identifiers for use on the Internet, including domain names, Internet Protocol (IP) addresses, application port numbers in the transport protocols, and many other parameters. Globally unified name spaces are essential for maintaining the global reach of the Internet. This role of ICANN distinguishes it as perhaps the only central coordinating body for the global Internet.

Services

Internet services include several useful tools and necessary elements for Internet users. These services extend beyond typical browsing and making websites available. The functions of these different services all combine to make the Internet function the way it does.

The **World Wide Web** (WWW) is an information space where documents and other web resources are identified by URLs, interlinked by hypertext links, and accessed via the Internet. It has become known simply as the Web. The World Wide Web was central to the development of the Information Age and is the primary tool billions of people use to interact on the Internet.

The **File Transfer Protocol** (FTP) is a standard network protocol used to transfer computer files between a client and server on a computer network (Figure 7). FTP is built on a client-server model architecture and uses separate control and data connections

Figure 6. Internet Corporation for Assigned Names and Numbers logo.

Figure 7.

between the client and the server. FTP users may authenticate themselves with a clear-text sign-in protocol, normally in the form of a username and password, but they can connect anonymously if the server is configured to allow it. For secure transmission that protects the username and password and encrypts the content, FTP is often secured with TLS/SSL (Transport Layer Security/Secure Sockets Layer). For more information about web security, see Chapter 8, "Security and Safety."

Usenet is a worldwide distributed discussion system. Users read and post messages — individually called "articles" or "posts" and collectively called "news" — to one or more categories, known as newsgroups. Usenet resembles a bulletin board system (BBS) in many respects and is the precursor to the Internet forums that are widely used today. Think of Usenet as a hybrid between email and web forums. Discussions are threaded into related messages, as with web forums and BBSs, though posts are stored on the server sequentially.

Telnet is an application layer protocol used on the Internet or on local area networks to provide a two-directional, interactive, text-oriented communication facility using a virtual terminal connection. User data are interspersed in-band with Telnet control information in an 8-bit byte-oriented data connection over the Transmission Control Protocol (TCP).

Voice over Internet Protocol (VoIP) is a methodology and group of technologies for the delivery of voice communications and multimedia sessions over Internet Protocol (IP) networks such as the Internet (Figure 8). Other terms commonly associated with VoIP are IP telephony, Internet telephony, broadband telephony, and broadband phone service.

Early providers of VoIP services offered business models and technical solutions that mirrored the architecture of the existing telephone network. Second-generation providers, such as Skype, have built closed networks for private user bases, offering the benefits of free calls and increased convenience while potentially charging for access to other communication networks, such as the public switched telephone network. This has limited the freedom of users to mix-and-match third-party hardware and software. Third-generation providers, such as Google Talk, have adopted the concept of federated VoIP, a departure from the architecture of the legacy networks. These solutions typically allow dynamic interconnection between users on any two domains on the Internet when a user wishes to place a call.

Figure 8. Video chat is an example of VoIP.

Electronic commerce, commonly called e-commerce, is the use of computer networks, such as the Internet, to trade or to facilitate trading in products or services (Figure 9). Electronic commerce draws on technologies such as mobile commerce, electronic funds transfer, supply chain management, Internet marketing, online transaction processing, electronic data interchange (EDI), inventory management systems, and automated data collection systems. Modern e-commerce typically uses the World Wide Web for at least one part of the transaction's life cycle, although it may also use other technologies such as email.

Figure 9. E-commerce shopping cart.

Protocols

For the Internet's many parts to function successfully, there must be a standardization of the way computers and networks communicate with one another. This standardization is achieved by creating and implementing various protocols, or rules and standards, across all functional connections to the Internet. The main protocols used are TCP/IP, IPv4, and IPv6, which together comprise nearly all Internet communications.

TCP/IP

The **Internet Protocol Suite** (TCP/IP) is the computer networking model and set of communications protocols used on the Internet and similar computer networks. It is commonly known as TCP/IP because its most important protocols, the Transmission Control Protocol (TCP) and the Internet Protocol (IP), were the first networking protocols defined in this standard. TCP/IP provides end-to-end connectivity specifying how data should be packetized, addressed, transmitted, routed, and received at the destination.

This functionality is organized into four abstraction layers which are used to sort all related protocols according to the scope of networking involved. The four layers are the application layer, the transport layer, the Internet layer, and the link layer. These are called layers because they sit on top of one another, and are described as a vertical stack of protocols.

The **application layer** is the scope within which applications create user data and communicate these data to other applications on the same host or another host. The applications, or processes, use the services provided by the underlying, lower layers, especially the transport layer, which provides pipes to other processes. The communication partners are characterized by the application architecture, such as the client-server model and peer-to-peer networking. The application layer is where all higher-level protocols, such as SMTP, FTP, SSH, and HTTP, operate. Processes are addressed via ports that essentially represent services.

The **transport layer** performs host-to-host communications on either the same or different hosts and on either the local network or remote networks separated by routers. This layer provides a channel for the communication needs of applications. UDP is the basic transport layer protocol, providing an unreliable datagram service. The Transmission Control Protocol provides flow-control, connection establishment, and reliable transmission of data.

The **Internet layer** has the task of exchanging datagrams across network boundaries. It provides a uniform networking interface that hides the actual topology or layout of the underlying network connections. It is therefore also referred to as the layer that establishes internetworking. Indeed, it defines and establishes the Internet. This layer defines the addressing and routing structures used for the TCP/IP protocol suite. The primary protocol in this scope is the Internet Protocol, which defines IP addresses. Its function in routing is to transport datagrams to the next IP router with connectivity to a network closer to the final data destination.

The **link layer** defines the networking methods within the scope of the local network link on which hosts communicate without intervening routers. This layer includes the protocols used to describe the local network topology and the interfaces needed to transmit Internet layer datagrams to next-neighbor hosts.

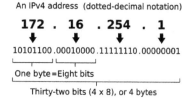

Figure 10. IPv4 is used on packet-switched networks.

IPv4

Internet Protocol version 4 (IPv4) is the fourth version of the Internet Protocol (Figure 10). It is one of the core protocols of standards-based internetworking methods for the Internet, and it was the first version used for the ARPANET in 1983. It still routes most Internet traffic today, despite the ongoing deployment of a successor protocol, IPv6.

IPv4 is a connectionless protocol for use on packet-switched networks. It operates on a best-effort delivery model, in that it does not guarantee delivery, nor does it assure proper sequencing or avoidance of duplicate delivery. These aspects of delivery are addressed instead by an upper layer transport protocol, such as the Transmission Control Protocol (TCP).

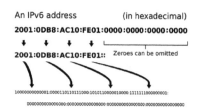

Figure 11. IPv6 is the most recent version the Internet Protocol.

IPv6

Internet Protocol version 6 (IPv6) is the most recent version of the Internet Protocol (Figure 11). IPv6 was developed by the Internet Engineering Task Force (IETF) to deal with the long-anticipated problem of IPv4 address exhaustion.

Every device on the Internet is assigned an IP address for identification and location definition. With the rapid growth of the Internet after commercialization in the 1990s, it became evident that far more addresses than those available in the IPv4 address space were necessary to connect new devices in the future. By 1998, the IETF had formalized the successor protocol.

IPv6 uses a 128-bit address, theoretically allowing 2^{128}, or approximately 3.4×10^{38} addresses. The actual number is slightly smaller, as multiple ranges are reserved for special use or completely excluded from use. The total number of possible IPv6 address is more than 7.9×10^{28} times as many as IPv4, which uses 32-bit addresses and provides approximately 4.3 billion addresses.

IPv6 provides other technical benefits in addition to a larger addressing space. It permits hierarchical address allocation methods for route aggregation across the Internet and thus limits the expansion of routing tables. The use of multicast addressing is expanded and simplified, and additional optimization is provided for the delivery of services. Device mobility, security, and configuration aspects have been considered in the design of the protocol.

IPv6 addresses are represented as eight groups of four hexadecimal digits with the groups being separated by colons — for example, 2001:0db8:0000:0042:0000:8a2e:0370:7334 — but there are methods to abbreviate this full notation.

2. Web Browsers

A web browser — often just called a browser — is a software application for retrieving, presenting, and traversing information resources on the World Wide Web (Figure 12).

Figure 12. A web browser.

A **Uniform Resource Identifier** (URI) identifies a resource by using a unique string of characters. This makes it possible for a web browser to interact with representations of the resource over a network, typically the World Wide Web, using specific protocols. A URL is a URI that, besides identifying a web resource, specifies how to act upon or obtain its representation — for example, it may specify both its primary access mechanism and its network location.

A **hyperlink** is a reference to data that the user can directly follow either by clicking or by hovering within the web browser (Figure 13). Each hyperlink points to a whole document or to a specific element within a document. Text with hyperlinks is called hypertext, and following hyperlinks is how you navigate or browse hypertext. The document containing a hyperlink is known as its source document. In an online reference work such as Wikipedia, for example, many words and terms in the text are hyperlinked to definitions of those terms.

Figure 13. A hyperlink is often used to reference data or redirect the reader.

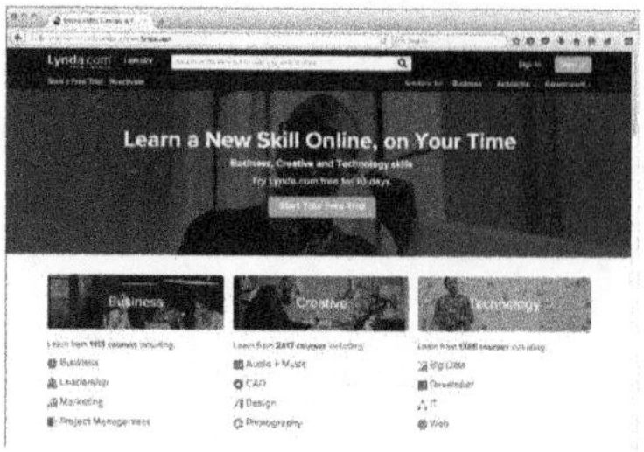

Figure 14. Plug-ins allow customization.

A **plug-in** — also known as an add-in or extension — is a software component that adds a specific feature to an existing computer program (Figure 14). With web browsers, plug-ins can add new features such as search engines, virus scanners, or the ability to use a new file type such as a new video format. Well-known browser plug-ins include the Adobe Flash Player, the QuickTime Player, and the Java plug-in, which can launch a user-activated Java applet on a web page to its execution on a local Java virtual machine. Browsers generally contain all the following elements from Table 1 in their interface.

The first web browser was invented in 1990 by Sir Tim Berners-Lee. Berners-Lee is the director of the World Wide Web Consortium (W3C), which oversees the Web's continued development, and he is also the founder of the World Wide Web Foundation. His browser was called WorldWideWeb and later renamed Nexus. In 1993, further browser software innovation by Marc Andreessen led to the release of Mosaic, the world's first popular browser, which made the World Wide Web system easy to use and more accessible to the average person. Andreessen's browser was one of the first graphical web browsers, and it sparked the Internet boom of the 1990s.

Microsoft responded with its Internet Explorer in 1995, initiating the industry's first "browser war." In 1998, Netscape launched what was to become the Mozilla Foundation in an attempt to produce a competitive browser using the open-source software model. That browser evolved into Firefox, which developed a respectable following. Apple's Safari had its first beta release in January 2003. As of April 2011, it had a dominant share of Apple-based web browsing.

The most recent major entrant to the browser market is Google Chrome, first released in September 2008. Chrome's use has increased significantly year by year, doubling its usage share from 8% to 16% by August 2011. This increase seems to be largely at the expense of Internet Explorer, whose share has tended to decrease from month to month. In December 2011, Chrome overtook Internet Explorer 8 as the most widely used web browser, but it still had lower usage than all versions of Internet Explorer combined. Chrome's user base continued to grow, however, and in May 2012, Chrome's usage passed that of all versions of Internet Explorer combined. By April 2014, Chrome's usage had hit 45%. Internet Explorer was de-emphasized in Windows 10, with Microsoft Edge replacing it as the default web browser.

3. World Wide Web

The terms "Internet" and "World Wide Web" are often used more or less interchangeably. However, the two are not the same. The Internet is a global system of interconnected computer networks. In contrast, the World Wide Web is just one of the services transferred over these networks. It is a collection of text documents and other resources, linked by hyperlinks and URLs, and usually accessed by web browsers.

Back and Forward Buttons	Used to go back to the previous resource and forward to the next	←
Refresh or Reload Button	Used to reload the current resource	C
Stop Button	Used to cancel loading the resource. In some browsers, the stop button is merged with the reload button	✕
Home Button	Used to return to the user's home page	⌂
Address Bar	Used to input the Uniform Resource Identifier (URI) of the desired resource and display it	
Status Bar	Used to display progres loading the resource and also the URI of liks when the cursor hovers over them, and page zooming capability	Connecting…
Viewport	The visible area of the web page within the browser window	
HTML View	The ability to view the HTML source for a page	

Table 1. Web browser elements.

Domain Names

A domain name is a string of text that defines a location where certain information or activities can be found on the Internet. Domain names are formed by the rules and procedures of the Domain Name System (DNS). Any name registered in the DNS is a domain name.

Domain names are used in various networking contexts and application-specific naming and addressing purposes. In general, a domain name represents an Internet Protocol (IP) resource, such as a personal computer used to access the Internet, a server computer hosting a website, the website itself, or any other service distributed via the Internet. Domain names identify Internet resources with a text-based label that is easier to memorize than the numerical addresses used in IPs. The domain name "whitehouse.gov," for example, is much easier to remember than the IP "104.125.236.54"

Domain names are used to establish a unique identity. Organizations can choose a domain name that corresponds to their name, helping Internet users to reach them easily. Today, the Internet Corporation for Assigned Names and Numbers (ICANN) manages the top-level development and architecture of the Internet domain namespace. It authorizes domain-name registrars to register and reassign domains. The domain namespace consists of a tree of domain names.

A domain name consists of one or more parts — technically called labels — that are conventionally presented without spacing, and separated by dots, such as "www.example.com". The rightmost label conveys the top-level domain. For example, the domain name "www.example.com" belongs to the top-level domain ".com." **Top-level domains** (TLDs) such as ".com," ".net," and ".org" are the highest level of domain names of the Internet. They form the root of the hierarchical Domain Name System. Every domain name ends with a top-level domain label.

Below the top-level domain in the domain-name hierarchy are the **second-level domain** (SLD) names. This is the name directly to the left of ".com" or other top-level domains. For example, in the domain "www.example.com," "example" is the second-level domain. SLDs are often created based on the name of a company, product, or service.

Below this level, the next domain-name component designates a particular host server. For example, with "www.example.com," the "www" identifies a World Wide Web server under the "example.com" domain. With "mail.example.com," the "mail" identifies an email server. Current technology allows multiple physical servers with either different or identical addresses to serve a single domain name, and also allows multiple domain names to be served by a single computer. The latter function is very popular in Web hosting service centers, where service providers host the websites of many organizations on just a few servers.

Many hostnames used for the World Wide Web begin with "www" because of the long-standing practice of naming Internet hosts according to the services they provide. The hostname of a web server is often "www," in the same way that it may be "ftp" for an FTP server, and "mail" for a mail server. However, the use of "www" is not required by any technical or policy standard, and not all websites use it. Many established websites still use the prefix, but others other subdomain names such as "www2," "secure," or "en." Many web servers are also set up so that both the main domain name — such as "example.com" — and the hostname with "www" — such as www.example.com — refer to the same IP address.

Websites

A website is a set of related web pages typically served from a single web domain. A website is hosted on at least one web server, accessible via a network such as the Internet or a private local area network through an Internet address known as a uniform resource locator (URL). All publicly accessible websites collectively make up the World Wide Web.

Most web pages contain **hyperlinks** to other related pages and sometimes to download-able files, source documents, definitions, and other web resources. A collection of useful, related resources interconnected via hypertext links thus becomes a "web" of information. Over time, many web resources connected to hyperlinks disappear, relocate, or are replaced with different content. This makes hyperlinks obsolete, a phenomenon known as "link rot," and the hyperlinks affected by it are often called "dead links."

Client-side scripts are often delivered with the web page, and these can make additional HTTP requests to the server — either in response to user actions such as mouse movements or clicks, or based on elapsed time. The server's responses modify the current page rather than creating a new page with each response, so the server needs only to provide limited, incremental information. This is called **dynamic updating**.

The **scheme specifiers** "http://" and "https://" at the start of a web URI specify the communication protocol to use for the request and response from a website. The HTTP protocol is fundamental to the operation of the World Wide Web, and the added encryption layer in HTTPS is essential when browsers send or retrieve confidential data, such as passwords or banking information. Usually, web browsers automatically put "http://" at the front of user-entered URIs if the user doesn't type it in.

Web Search Engines

A web search engine is a software system designed to search for information on the World Wide Web (Figure 15) The search results are usually presented in a list that is referred to as search engine results pages. The information may be a mix of web pages, images, and other types of files. Some search engines also mine data available in databases or open directories. Unlike web directories, which are maintained only by human editors, search engines also maintain real-time information by running an algorithm on a web crawler.

Figure 15. A search engine.

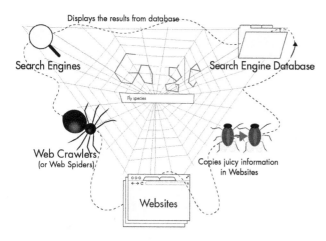

Figure 16. How web crawling works.

Web search engines get their information by **web crawling** from site to site (Figure 16). This is done by a "spider" program that checks for the standard filename "robots.txt," addressed to it. It then sends certain information back to be indexed depending on many factors, such as titles, page content, JavaScript, and Cascading Style Sheets (CSS). Other factors may be headings, as shown by the standard HTML markup of the informational content, or the content's metadata in HTML meta tags. Meta tags are data tags that provide structured metadata about a web page.

Indexing means associating words and other definable tokens found on web pages to their domain names and HTML-based fields (Figure 17). The associations are made in a public database that is available for web search queries. A query from a user could be a single word, if desired. The index helps find information relating to the query as quickly as possible.

Full-text Search Index

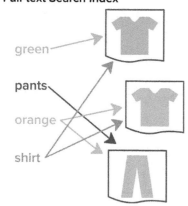

Figure 17. Indexes work by categorizing words or tokens.

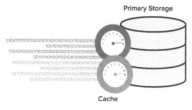

Figure 18. Cached content aides loading speeds.

The cached version of a page is some or all of the content needed to render it. **Caching** happens between visits by the spider. The cached version of a page stored in the search engine's working memory is quickly sent to an inquirer (Figure 18). If a visit is overdue, the search engine can simply act as a web proxy instead. In this case, the page may differ from the search terms indexed. The cached page holds the appearance of the version whose words were indexed, so a cached version of a page can be useful to the website when the actual page has been lost.

Typically, when a user engages in **searching** by typing a query into a search engine, the query is a few keywords. The index already has the names of the sites containing the keywords, and these are instantly obtained from the index. The real processing load is in generating the web pages that are the search results list. Every page in the entire list must be weighted according to information in the indexes. Then the top search result item requires the lookup, reconstruction, and markup of the snippets showing the context of the keywords matched. These are only part of the processing required by each search-results web page. Further pages require more of this post-processing.

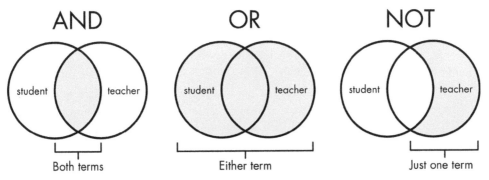

Figure 19. Boolean operators.

Beyond simple keyword lookups, search engines offer their own GUI- or command-driven operators and search parameters to refine the search results. These provide the necessary controls for the user engaged in a feedback loop. Users create a feedback loop by filtering and weighting while refining the search results, given the initial pages of the first search results. For example, since 2007 the google.com search engine has allowed users to filter by date by clicking "Show search tools" in the leftmost column of the initial search results page, and then selecting the desired date range. It's also possible to weight by date because each page has a modification time.

Most search engines support the use of **boolean operators** — "and," "or," and "not" — to help end users refine the search query. Boolean operators are used for literal searches that allow the user to refine and extend the terms of the search (Figure 19). The engine looks for the words or phrases exactly as entered. Putting "and" between two search terms means the search will only return results that contain both those terms. Putting "or" between two terms means the search will return all results that contain either one of the terms. And putting "not" between two terms means the search will return only results that contain the first term and not the second.

Some search engines provide an advanced feature called proximity search, which allows users to define the distance between keywords. There is also concept-based searching where the research involves using statistical analysis on pages containing the words or phrases you search for. Also, there are natural-language queries that allow the user to type a question in the same form one would ask it to a human.

Levels of the Web

The **surface web** — also called the visible web, clearnet, indexed web, indexable web or light-net — is the portion of the World Wide Web that is readily available to the general public and searchable with standard web search engines. The surface web is all the web content that has been indexed by search engines. According to one source, as of June, 2015, Google's index of the surface web contains about 14.5 billion pages.

The **deep web** — also called deepnet, invisible web, and hidden web — is made up of parts of the World Wide Web whose contents are not indexed by standard search engines for any reason (Table 2). The deep web includes many common uses such as web mail and online banking, but it also includes paid-for services with a paywall such as video-on-demand. Sometimes web content may not be indexed because content varies for those with different levels of access, because certain pages only come up in response to a submitted query or form, or because a page contains content in file formats not handled by search engines. The size of the deep web is unknown, but some researchers estimate that it consists of about 7.5 petabytes — or 7,500 terabytes — of data.

The **dark web** is the World Wide Web content that exists on darknets. These are networks that use the public Internet but require specific software, configurations or authorization for access (Table 3). The dark web only forms a small part of the deep web, but sometimes the term "deep web" is used to refer more specifically to the dark web.

The darknets that constitute the dark web include small, friend-to-friend and peer-to-peer networks and larger, popular networks like Freenet, I2P, and Tor, which are operated by public organizations. Users of the dark web refer to the regular web as the clearnet because of its unencrypted nature. The Tor dark web may be referred to as onionland, a reference to the network's top-level domain suffix, "onion," and the traffic anonymization technique of onion routing.

How much of the dark web is used for illicit purposes is debatable, but it has the potential to be used for both legal and illegal reasons. Content varies from blogs and forums, for users who simply want additional privacy, to sites for money laundering, weapons sales, drug sales, hacking services, and pornography. Rumors of assassination services available on the deep web seem to be an urban legend rather than reality. The encrypted nature of the dark web lends itself to all kinds of extreme speculation about its content but the reality is often more mundane.

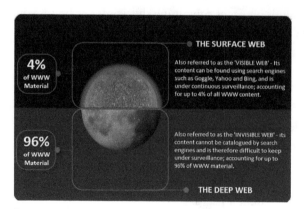

Figure 20. Most content online is not searchable.

Figure 21. Tor allows dark web users to search for ".onion" sites.

A further level of the Web is an **overlay network**, which is a computer network built on top of another network. Nodes in the overlay network are connected by virtual or logical links. Each corresponds to a path, perhaps through many physical links, in the underlying network. For example, distributed systems such as peer-to-peer networks and client-server applications are overlay networks because their nodes run on top of the Internet.

Contextual Web	Pages with content that varies for different access contexts (e.g., ranges of client IP addresses or previous navigation sequence)
Dynamic Content	Dynamic pages which are returned in response to a submitted query or accessed only through a form, especially if open-domain input elements (such as text fields) are used — such fields are hard to navigate without domain knowledge
Limited Access Content	Sites that limit access to their pages in a technical way — e.g., using the Robots Exclusion Standard or CAPTCHAs, or no-store directives which prohibit search engines from browsing them and creating cached copies
Non-HTML/Text Content	Textual content encoded in multimedia (image or video) files or specific file formats not handled by search engines
Private Web	Sites that require registration and login (password-protected resources)
Scripted Content	Pages that are only accessible through links provided by JavaScript, as well as content dynamically downloaded from Web servers via Flash or Ajax solutions
Software	Certain content is intentionally hidden from the regular Internet, accessible only with special software, such as Tor, I2P, or other darknet software — for example, Tor allows users to access websites using the ".onlion" host suffix anonymously, hiding their IP address
Unlinked Content	Pages that are not linked to by other pages, which may prevent web crawling programs from accessing the content. This content is also referred to as pages without backlinks (also known as inlinks). Also, search engines do not always detect all backlinks from searched webpages
Web Archives	Web archival services such as the Wayback Machine enable users to see archived versions of webs pages across time, including websites which have become inaccessible, and are not indexed by search engines such as Google

Table 2. Type of deep web content.

Botnets	Botnets are often structured with their command and control servers based on a censorship-resistant hidden service, creating a large amount of bot-related traffic.
Bitcoin Services	Bitcoin services such as tumblers are often available on Tor, and some offer darknet market integration.
Darknet Markets	Commercial darknet markets, which mediate transactions for illegal drugs and other goods, attracted significant media coverage starting with the popularity of Silk Road and its subsequent seizure by legal authorities. Other markets sell software exploits and weapons.
Hacking Groups and Services	Many hackers sell their services individually or as a part of groups. Such groups include hackforum, Trojanforge, Mazafaka, dark0de and the TheRealDeal darknet market. Some have been known to track and extort apparent pedophiles.
Fraud Services	There are numerous carding forums, as well as fraud and counterfeiting services. Many such sites are scams themselves.
Hoaxes and Unverified Content	There are reports of crowd-funded assassinations and hitmen for hire. However, these are believed to be exclusively scams.
Phishing and Scams	Phishing attempts via cloned websites and other scam sites are numerous, with darknet markets often advertised with fraudulent URLs.
Puzzles	Puzzles such as Cicada 3301 and successors will sometimes use hidden services in order to more anonymously provide clues, often increasing speculation as to the identity of their creators.
Illegal and Ethically Disputed Pornography	There is regular law-enforcement action against sites distributing child pornography — often via compromising the site by distributing malware to the users. Sites use complex systems of guides, forums and community regulation.
Terrorism	There are at least some real and fraudulent websites claiming to be used by ISIL, including a fake one seized in Operation Onymous. In the wake of the November 2015 Paris attacks, an actual such site was hacked by an Anonymous affiliated hacker group GhostSec and replaced with an ad for Prozac.

Table 3. Types of dark web content.

Chapter 8
Security and Safety

"Security" in our daily lives means safety from danger or threats. Computer security, also known as cyber security or IT security, provides that same kind of safety for computers. Effective security protects your computer's hardware, software, and stored information from theft or damage. It protects you by preventing outside access to your computer's hardware and software by physical means or through network access, data and code injection, or malpractice.

The importance of computer security is growing because of our increasing reliance on computer systems and "smart" devices such as smartphones and televisions that connect to networks. In addition, networks — not just the Internet and private data networks but also Bluetooth, public Wi-Fi, and other wireless networks — keep us connected to computers all the time. In a world that's always connected, we need to be constantly guarding against weaknesses that expose our personal information.

However, fighting cybercrime is very challenging work. First, identifying attackers is difficult because they often operate through proxies and from far away. Hackers also take measures to remain anonymous, and if they successfully breach security, they are often able to delete any logs to cover their tracks. Second, the sheer number of attempted attacks is so large that organizations can't spend time pursuing each attacker. Most of these attacks are made by automated programs like vulnerability scanners and computer worms, so there isn't even a person to trace back to.

Law enforcement also faces many challenges. Officers are often unfamiliar with the technology, and training can be expensive, so most lack the skills or interest in pursuing cyber-attackers. In addition, identifying attackers across a network can require logs from various points in the network and in many different countries. The release of these records to law enforcement requires a search warrant unless they are voluntarily surrendered by a network administrator or a system administrator. Depending on the circumstances, any legal proceedings can be drawn out past the point when records have been regularly destroyed or the information is no longer relevant.

What this means is that computer security falls mostly to users and network administrators. This work comes down to three main activities — preventing threats, detecting intrusions, and responding to danger. However, relatively few organizations maintain effective detection systems for their data, and fewer still have organized response procedures in place. That means that in most cases, computer security is achieved mainly by preventing threats to your own computer.

This chapter introduces you to basic security concerns and then explains what you as a user can do to safeguard your computer. It ends with a closer look at how cryptography works to secure information.

Figure 1.

1. Malware

The words "malicious software" have been shortened to "**malware**," and this term refers to many different types of applications — viruses, Trojan horses, spyware, computer worms, and so on (Figure 2) — that break into your computer and cause harm. A computer **virus** used to refer to *any* malicious software, because it "infects" a system and makes it difficult or impossible for that system to function normally — just like a virus infects a human immune system. These viruses replicate their structures or effects by infecting other files on a computer. The purpose is generally to take over the computer and steal data or do other harmful things.

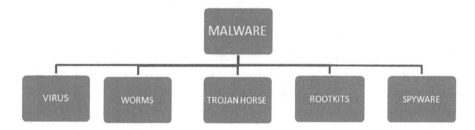

Figure 2. Types of Malware.

However, the simple term "virus" doesn't begin to cover the software that cybercriminals have devised over the years. Computer **worms**, for example, are like viruses but replicate themselves throughout a computer network. Unlike a virus, though, worms don't require human intervention or directives from the malware author to spread. Many other types of malicious programs also break into computers and cause trouble.

Ransomware is a type of malware that restricts access to the computer system it infects and then demands a ransom be paid to the creator of the malware for the restriction to be removed. This restriction might come in the form of simply locking the victim's device, or it might be as complicated as encrypting all of the victim's files. With either ransomware or crypto-ransomware, however, paying the hackers seldom results in getting access to your computer again.

Scareware accomplishes its goals by warning the user about a serious problem and offering to sell the solution. The selling approach uses social engineering to cause shock, anxiety, or the perception of a threat, generally directed at an unsuspecting user. The user pays for the software, which might be marketed as a fix, only to find that it does nothing.

Spyware refers to programs that monitor activity on a computer system and report that information to others without the user's consent. This sometimes takes the form of advertising pop-up windows. If the user interacts with those windows, the spyware reports back information about the user without the user knowing about it. **Key-loggers** are programs that record a user's typed keystrokes without the user's knowledge. This can be used for stealing passwords and other personal information.

A **Trojan horse**, or Trojan, refers to malicious software that pretends to be harmless so that a user willingly allows it to be downloaded onto the computer. Its malicious intent only becomes obvious when it is already too late.

A **botnet** is a network of "zombie" computers that have been infected and then taken over by an automated robot, or bot, and is controlled by a "bot-master" or "bot-herder." Botnets perform large-scale malicious acts — such as data mining or making massive calculations needed for hacking — for the creator of the botnet. Botnets are often used to send spam or to provide hackers with unrestricted access to targeted users' computers. They're also used to perpetrate distributed denial of service (DDOS) attacks against webhosts.

A **rootkit** is a particularly dangerous type of malware designed to hide its presence on the host operating system through stealth. **Rootkits** enable malicious activity by spyware and other more obvious forms of malware while remaining undetected in the system. Once the system has been compromised, sometimes by changing or replacing vital programs, it becomes embedded in what appear to be system files. As a result, once a rootkit has gained access to a computer, it's very hard to track it down and get rid of it.

While malware is designed to be unobtrusive to the user with the infected computer, there are a few ways to be alerted that your computer may have a virus:

- If you frequently hear your hard drive start working when you aren't running any programs and your system isn't doing any updates, it's possible that a virus is working in the background.

- If your computer suddenly starts taking much longer than usual to boot up, a virus might be causing the slowdown.

- If you can't log into Windows with your correct login information, it's likely that your login process has been affected by a virus.

- If random advertisements and unexplainable error messages suddenly start to pop up or windows open up and you aren't able to close them, it's likely your computer is infected.

These malware programs are the main enemies in the fight to secure your computer. Fortunately, there are many things you can do to prevent malware from breaking into your computer or computing device. Web security is also possible by improving your own network's security, understanding and using cryptography, and relying on the widespread use of Internet Protocols online.

2. Password Security

When users surf the Internet for information, check their email, shop online, read online newspapers, or post messages on Facebook, they aren't necessarily thinking about the security of their connections. The Internet has made all of these activities easier and faster, but this convenience comes with a price — whenever you connect to a network, you expose yourself to security risks.

The most common type of security is a password. When you use any service that saves sensitive data — even as simple as your name — it probably asks you to set up a password. The widespread use of passwords online means we need to remember a lot of them, and most people have some kind of system for remembering their password (Figure 3). Saving passwords, sharing passwords, using easy-to-remember passwords, and using the same password for everything are all convenient, of course, but they all expose you to a greater security risk.

This section will look at the first line of defense — passwords — and how to use them securely.

Figure 3. A strong password helps protect you online.

Creating Your Password

Before looking at how to create secure passwords, it's important to understand how passwords are hacked so that you can avoid the pitfalls and practice good password management. There are generally five tried and true ways to hack a password:

- Asking or social engineering are easily the most common ways to access someone's password. People will usually give their passwords to family, friends and co-workers upon being asked. A good social engineer, someone who is practiced in the art of manipulating people so they give up confidential information, can usually trick someone into revealing a password.

- Guessing is the second most common method of hacking passwords. Most people choose passwords that are easy to remember, and those words are usually related to the person — the names of family members or pets, street names, birthdays, favorite things — or incredibly obvious, like using the word "password" or the "qwerty" pattern from a standard keyboard.

- Brute force is another method of hacking passwords. A hacker simply tries to sign in using thousands or millions of different passwords, one at a time. If you have a simple password such as "cat," for example, a hacker will attempt to sign-in starting with "aaa", "aab," "aac," and will continue this pattern until the hacker gets to "cat." The only thing to stop brute-force attacks is a longer and more complex password.

- Common-word attacks are a simple type of brute-force hack. Instead of trying combinations of letters, the hacker uses common words to bypass security. The longer the word, then, the harder a password is to hack.

- Dictionary attacks are the fifth typical method of hacking passwords. People will often use common words or combinations of words for a password. Hackers will use full dictionaries from a number of languages and combine words to crack your password. Complexity and length will once again frustrate these types of hacks.

The time it takes to crack a password is also an important consideration. Using only lowercase letters, there are 17,576 (26^3) possible combinations for a three-letter password like "cat." That's not too hard to crack with hacking software. If you include an uppercase letter with the same word — "caT" — the number of combinations increases to 308,915,776 (26^6). With specialized hacking software, that's still pretty easy to crack, but it will take the hacker longer to do so. The longer and more complex the password, then, the longer it will take hackers to break in.

Following these guidelines will make your passwords harder to figure out:

- Use a minimum of 12 to 20 characters, if permitted.

- Include lowercase and uppercase letters, numbers, and typographic symbols — !, @, #, $, %, ^, &, or * — if permitted.

- Generate passwords randomly whenever possible. Online and software tools will help you with this.

- Don't use the same password in different user accounts or software systems. You can't always avoid this because some organizations require that you use the same password for several different systems within this organization. This is where a really strong password is needed.

- Don't repeat characters and avoid keyboard patterns, actual words, letter or number sequences, usernames, names of pets or people, or biographical information.

- Don't use information that is or could become publicly associated with you or your account. Social engineers scour social media sites harvesting information about future victims.

- Don't use information that your colleagues or acquaintances might know about you.

- If memorizing passwords is difficult for you, you can use words if you mix uncommon words in nonsensical patterns like "AmberMuskrat." You can also increase the complexity by replacing "e" with "3" and or "$" for "s" and by adding a number or character on either end, such as with "!Amb3rMu$krat8." Increase the complexity even more by using at least three words like "fluffyisstuffy."

- You can also use a phonetic password where the pattern sounds like a word — making it easier to remember — but isn't actually a word — making it harder to hack. Examples would be something like "jojubopolo" or "mihimamu." Again, you can add a non-letter or a number or two to make it a stronger password.

Common practice suggests that using the mix of uncommon words in nonsensical patterns would still be susceptible to common-word and dictionary attacks and easily hacked. However, as Table 1 shows, even if a hacker uses specialized software that can process 100 password requests per second, "fluffyisstuffy" isn't such a bad password after all.

Type of Password	Password	Method of Attack	Time to Complete
6 random letters	kqdhyr	brute-force	1 month
6 characters, including 2 numbers	kqdh36	brute-force	8 months
6 characters, with upper and lower case, numbers, and symbols	K3qd*r	brute-force	200+ years
6 letter common word	kitten	common word	3–4 minutes
2 common words	kittenmittens	common word	2 months
3 common words	warmkittenmittens	common word	2,500+ years
3 uncommon words	fluffyisstuffy	dictionary	38+ million years
5 uncommon words	baconfluffyisstuffymorning	dictionary	500+ billion years

Table 1. How long it takes to hack different types of passwords at 100 attempts per second.

Using Your Passwords

Saving your passwords is another security concern. Some guidelines advise against writing passwords down. However, because you have to access so many password-protected systems, others encourage you to write down your passwords on paper but then make sure that the written password list is kept in a safe place. Don't attach it to your computer's monitor or leave it in an unlocked desk drawer.

The worst password is the one you forget. A reasonable compromise for using large numbers of passwords is to record them in a password manager. These are available as stand-alone applications such as KeePass, web browser extensions such as LastPass, or managers built into the operating system such as Apple's iCloud Keychain. Don't allow your browser to save passwords. Not only can others with access to your computer see you log files, but if your computer is stolen, the thief can access your usernames, passwords and even credit card information very easily. A password manager can record hundreds of different passwords, but the user only has to remember a single password that opens the encrypted password database when prompted. Needless to say, this single password should be strong and well-protected, not recorded anywhere.

Most password managers can also create strong random passwords using a secure random password generator. To access these passwords, you only have to remember a single password that opens the encrypted password database when prompted. Needless to say, this single password should be strong and well-protected, and you should not write it down anywhere, even on paper. Most password managers also have a function that can automatically create strong random passwords using a secure random password generator. Since password managers are a security tool, most good ones also provide functions that resist other threats we describe later, such as key-logging and clipboard logging.

How you use passwords online is also a security concern. When you're using the Internet, how can you be sure that your identity, passwords, personal information, shopping information, and credit card numbers are all protected? Here are some tips for using passwords carefully while online:

- Never give your username and password to anyone.

- Always make sure you read the privacy policy of the websites that you visit before giving them any personal information.

- If you are shopping online, never shop from an untrusted website. The first step is to make sure the URL starts with HTTPS. The "S" stands for "secure." This means all communications between your browser and the website are encrypted. If you have doubts about the website, check its privacy policy for information about its method of protecting your data. If it's not available, or if you are still in doubt, don't shop from that website and search for more trusted websites to do your shopping.

- Don't give your email username and password to websites that will be able to log on to your account automatically. This is a big risk since personal information can be accessed through other emails.

- It's helpful to think of your password as a code. If you're trying to protect your information with a code, it's best to create a code that is tough or impossible to crack, right? Studying and designing codes is called cryptography, and is discussed in more detail later in this chapter. For now, we encourage you to create passwords more like a code than like a secret phrase or word, since those can be cracked more easily.

3. Computer Security

Other common computing behaviors expose your computing devices to risk. This includes actions like clicking "accept" on every web notification, opening files without virus-scanning them first, and clicking links without being sure they take you where you expect to go. These habits are more convenient than double-checking everything you do, but again, just one lapse in your computer security can be exploited, and one time can cause a lot of problems. This section will help you to make sure that all your computing devices are secure.

Desktop and Laptop Security

With security safeguards, it's a good idea to start by learning about the **vulnerabilities** that are most relevant to your situation. If you know what they are, you can then take action against them. A vulnerability is a system flaw in danger of being exploited. Many vulnerabilities are documented in the Common Vulnerabilities and Exposures (CVE) database, used by security developers to close gaps in security for users. The actions you can take as an individual user are keeping software up-to-date, using firewalls, and installing additional security software on your computer.

Figure 4.

Operating systems that provide regular **software updates** frequently release fixes for various vulnerabilities as they arise. Keeping your computer's software up-to-date is a key factor in maintaining its security (Figure 4).

A **firewall** is a network security system that monitors and controls network traffic based on predetermined security rules. It can be implemented as software running on the machine (Figure 5). Another implementation is a so-called physical firewall which consists of a separate computer whose only job is to filter network traffic before it reaches the user's machine. Firewalls are

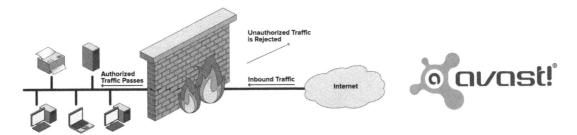

Figure 5. How a firewall works.   **Figure 6.** Avast is an antivirus software.

commonly used in machines permanently connected to the Internet. Most modern machines run both types of firewall, one in your modem and one in your computer's operating system.

Antivirus software is the most commonly used application security software. Antivirus software, sometimes known as anti-malware software, is computer software used to prevent, detect, and remove malicious software. Antivirus software was originally developed to detect and remove computer viruses, hence the name. However, with the growth of other kinds of malware, antivirus software has expanded to provide protection from other computer threats such as browser hijackers, ransomware, key-loggers, backdoors, rootkits, Trojan horses, worms, malicious LSPs, dialers, fraud tools, adware, and spyware (Figure 6).

Tablet and Mobile Phone Security

An important aspect of many mobile devices is open-platform functionality. This means that anyone with the right tools and knowledge can develop software applications for a particular device. This kind of platform openness is expected to keep increasing in the future as part of the democratization of technology, and it's is a large part of why mobile devices are so convenient. However, with convenience comes increased risk. Unknown or untrusted apps can use this openness to gain access to mobile resources and cause damage to the user, device, network, or all three if they aren't blocked by suitable security and network precautions.

Antivirus software and firewalls are one precaution. Antivirus software can be run on a mobile device to verify that it is not infected by any known malware threat. A firewall can check whether installed applications are seeking to establish suspicious types of communication. You can also control how you allow apps to use **global positioning system** (GPS) settings and access privileges that you grant to each of your installed apps. Most mobile devices will prompt users to accept any attempts by apps to use GPS data or gain privileges to make changes to your data. You should be very careful about what you choose to accept when prompted to make these decisions.

Figure 7.

Most mobile devices now contain GPS capability that records a user's exact geographical location (Figure 7). Due to the popularity of GPS devices, users' privacy has become a subject of debate. Some people think a user's location is private information, and should not be available to view without legal approval.

This ability to pinpoint a user's exact location helps with location-based advertising. Advertisers using mobile marketing might promote stores near the user instead of distant ones. The advertising agency also records users' locations for future use, such as sending emails to remind users of their purchase the next time they are nearby. Since GPS data are not currently considered legally "private," some think that advertising based on location is troubling because marketing agencies and corporations can use your location data with or without your consent. Even more troubling is imagining the potential for harm if this information got into the wrong hands. Individuals with malicious physical intent could use their victim's GPS data to predict location at any given time, increasing the risk of harm.

If you unthinkingly approve whatever privilege permissions a new app asks for, that blanket approval could very well expose your private data to marketing groups that work with the app's developers. For example, if an app asks to access your contacts, think about why the app developers would want that information. Could they use it to create phone call lists for unwanted marketing calls? It's possible. Be careful what you agree to when accepting access privilege requests from apps and consider just what the potential consequences are.

Virtual Private Network

A **virtual private network** (VPN) is another tool that can provide a certain level of security, especially with mobile Internet devices. A VPN is a network connection that enables you to create a secure connection to another location, thereby allowing you to appear as if you were in another place. A VPN extends a private network across a public network and enables users to send and receive data across shared or public networks as if their computing devices were directly connected to the private network.

Normally, when you connect to the Internet, you first connect to your Internet Service Provider (ISP), which then connects you to websites or other Internet resources. All your Internet traffic passes through your ISP's servers and can be viewed by your ISP. When you use a VPN, you connect to a VPN server run by your VPN provider via an encrypted connection. This means that all data traveling between your computer and the VPN server is encrypted so that only you and the VPN server can see it.

This setup has a number of important benefits. First, your ISP can't see your data because they are encrypted. Second, the ISP doesn't know which websites you visit because all Internet

VPN

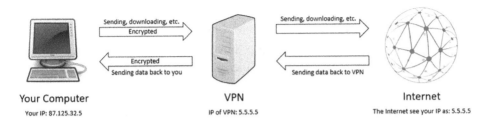

Figure 8. How VPNs hide your IP from the internet.

activity is routed through the VPN server. Your ISP can only see that you are connected to the VPN server (Figure 8).

If the VPN server is located in a different country — and most VPN services run servers in many different countries — then as far as the Internet is concerned, you're also located in that country. Anyone monitoring your activity from the Internet will only be able to trace it back to the VPN server. Unless the VPN provider hands over your details, your real IP address remains hidden. This allows you to circumvent any geo-restrictions and censorship by school, work, ISP, or government and "geo-spoof" your location in order to access any services denied to you based on your geographical location.

VPNs also provide data security so that even if network traffic is attacked at the packet level, the attacker will only see encrypted data. When using public Wi-Fi hotspots, the Internet connection between your device and the VPN server is encrypted, so even if a hacker manages to intercept your Wi-Fi data, the data are safe because they are encrypted. Most VPNs also provide message integrity to detect any instances of tampering with transmitted messages.

VPNs provide privacy, but they do not make you anonymous. The VPN provider will always know who you are and can see what you are doing on the Internet. However, privacy-oriented VPN services go to great lengths to protect their customers' privacy. By using a VPN, you shift your trust away from your ISP, which has no interest in or commitment to protecting your privacy, to the VPN provider, which usually promises to protect your privacy.

When choosing a VPN service, you should consider more than just the price of the service. You should also consider the technical measures that a service uses to prevent hackers or governments from forcing access to your data. If it keeps logs of activity, for example, that could impact your privacy. VPN client software should not only look good and be easy to use but offer useful features such as VPN kill switches and DNS leak protection. It should use encryption protocols that are still in use and not outdated.

Beyond privacy protections, there are other things you may want to consider:

- Number of servers: If you need to connect to servers located all over the place, then the more the better — and the more likely it is that a server will be located where you want it to be.

- Number of simultaneous connections: Some providers only let you connect one device at a time while others allow you to connect your PC, laptop, phone, Xbox, and tablet all at once.

- Customer support: Many VPN users are still learning the ropes, so look for customer support that actually answers your questions in a reasonable timeframe, and knows what it's talking about.

- Free trials and money-back guarantees: The best way to decide if a service is for you is to try it before you buy it.

3. Network and Cloud Security

Network security is the set of policies and procedures adopted to monitor which devices can access networks. This kind of security prevents unauthorized access, misuse, modification, or unintended denial of access to a computer network and network-accessible resources. Network security does as its title explains: It secures the network by protecting and overseeing network operations. The most common and simple way of protecting a network resource is by assigning it a unique name and a corresponding password.

The authorization of access to data in a network is controlled by the network administrator. Users choose or are assigned an ID and password or other authenticating information that allows them access to information and programs within their authority. This is as simple as setting up a password-protected method for accessing your network.

Network security covers a variety of computer networks, both public and private, that are used to conduct transactions and communications among businesses, government agencies and individuals. Networks can be private, such as those within a company, and others might be open to public access.

The most common type of protection used in personal Wi-Fi networks is the Wi-Fi Protected Access (WPA) security protocol. Most home network routers have WPA and second-generation WPA2 security capabilities. This appears to users as a simple password login to access the network, but is actually a fairly complex and strong security protocol that, when paired with a long enough password that follows the guidelines for passwords in this chapter (14 or more random characters), is virtually impossible to crack.

Cloud Security

Cloud computing is one of the newest and most exciting technologies that now support mobile and flexible computing. This term refers to the storage of data on servers in remote locations that are known collectively as "the cloud." These storage locations offer great flexibility to users who access their data from multiple locations (Figure 9). Cloud users should consider the security of information they share on the cloud just as carefully as they guard information stored anywhere else. Remember, the Cloud is just someone else's computer, and all computers are susceptible to being hacked. Cloud security refers to a broad set of policies, technologies, and controls deployed to protect data, applications, and the associated infrastructure of cloud computing. Fortunately, developers creating cloud systems have created security structures unique to the cloud based on technology similar to other systems.

Figure 9.

Deterrent controls are intended to reduce attacks on a cloud system. Much like a "keep out" warning sign on a fence, deterrent controls typically reduce the threat level by informing potential attackers that there will be adverse consequences for them if they proceed.

Preventive controls strengthen the system against threats, generally by reducing if not actually eliminating vulnerabilities. Strong authentication of cloud users, for instance, makes it less likely that unauthorized users can access cloud systems and more likely that cloud users are positively identified.

Detective controls detect and respond appropriately to any incidents that occur. In the event of an attack, a detective control will signal the preventive or corrective controls to address the issue. Cloud systems typically use system and network security monitoring, including intrusion detection and prevention arrangements to detect attacks.

Corrective controls come into effect during or after a security incident to reduce the consequences of that incident. Restoring system backups in order to rebuild a compromised system is an example of a corrective control.

The simplest way to keep your cloud data safe from harm is to create **backup** versions of all your cloud-stored data. This can be done fairly simply by setting backup schedules in your operating system utilities, or by maintaining your own schedule of regular backup activities to additional storage drives (Figure 10).

Figure 10.

4. Basic Internet Security Protocols

A lot of web security happens without our knowing about it. The cryptography that keeps our connections secure is built into our web browsers so that we can safely and privately use the Internet. Decades of work by software developers have resulted in a set of browser use protocols called **transport layer security** (TLS) and its predecessor, **secure sockets layer** (SSL). Both are frequently referred to as "SSL," and both are cryptography protocols designed to provide security over a computer network. Several versions of these protocols are in widespread use in applications such as web browsing, email, Internet faxing, instant messaging, and voice-over-IP (VoIP).

Major websites use TLS to secure all communications between their servers and web browsers. The TLS protocol allows client-server software to communicate over a network without eavesdropping or tampering. Since protocols can operate either with or without TLS

Figure 11. A digital handshake.

(or SSL), the client browser initiates the setup of a TLS connection with the server. There are two main ways of achieving this. One option is to use a different port number for TLS connections. For example, HTTPS, a common TLS protocol, uses port 443 for all its connections. The other option is for the client to use a protocol-specific mechanism like STARTTLS, which is used for mail and news protocols, to request that the server switch its connection to TLS (Figure 11).

Once the client and server have agreed to use TLS, they negotiate a connection by using a handshaking procedure. This name comes from the old idea that business transactions should end with a handshake to show agreement. Client-server connections "shake hands" as a sign of their agreement to communicate securely.

During the handshake, the client and server agree on various parameters used to establish the connection's security. The handshake begins when a client connects to a TLS-enabled server, requesting a secure connection, and presents a list of supported ciphers and hash functions. From this list, the server picks a cipher and hash function that it also supports and notifies the client of the decision. Next, the server usually sends back its identification in the form of a digital certificate. The certificate contains the server name, the trusted certificate authority (CA), and the server's public encryption key. The client confirms the validity of the certificate before proceeding.

The session keys used for the secure connection are then generated by the client. There are two ways for the client to do this: One option is for the client to encrypt a random number with the server's public key and send the result to the server. The server can then decrypt with its private key. Both parties then use the random number to generate a unique session key for subsequent encryption and decryption of data during the session. The other option is for the client to use a Diffie-Hellman key exchange to securely generate a random and unique session key for encryption and decryption that has "forward secrecy." This means that even if the server's private key is made public in the future, it cannot be used to decrypt the current session — even if the session is intercepted and recorded.

This concludes the handshake and begins the secured connection, which is encrypted and decrypted with the session key until the connection closes. If any one of the above steps fail, the TLS handshake fails, and the connection is not created.

5. Cryptography

Information cryptography uses ciphers — or keys — to both lock and unlock information in the interest of keeping it secure (Figure 12). Locking is called **encryption**, and the key is used to encipher information. Unlocking is called **decryption**, and the key is used to decipher information. Depending on the kind of cryptography used, the key that enciphers may also be used to decipher, or a different key may be used to decipher.

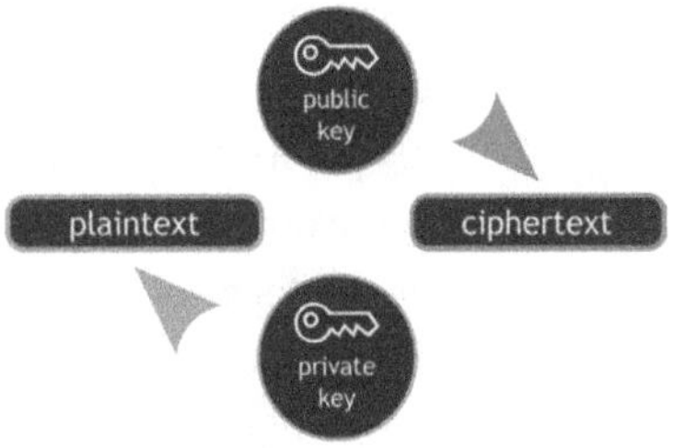

There are several types of encryption. Full-disk encryption automatically encrypts anything saved to your hard drive. File encryption encrypts files on a case-by-case basis. End-to-end (E2E) encryption obscures the content of messages so they can only be read by the sender and receiver. Encryption involves a lot of secrecy, but when the information that you save to your disk or send online is sensitive — name, birthdate, credit card numbers — good encryption methods ensure that you can keep your private information secret from others. Good encryption schemas help enforce five concepts important to security — confidentiality, integrity, authentication, availability, and nonrepudiation.

Figure 12. Cryptography uses clphers, or keys to lock and unlock information.

Confidentiality means that only the people who are authorized to view information should have access to it. Cryptography has traditionally been used to protect data, but not resources. Resources are usually protected through limiting information by using firewalls, for example, or address translation mechanisms.

Integrity is the assurance that a file does not change during transit. Cryptography provides mechanisms for detecting violations of integrity but not preventing them. It can use a digital signature, for example, to determine if any data have changed.

Authentication is the assurance regarding the identity of the person at the other end of message transit. Authentication stops imposters.

Availability means that the information must be available when needed. The systems used to store and process the information, the security controls used to protect it, and the communication channels used to access it must be functioning correctly.

Nonrepudiation means that users cannot repudiate — deny — that they sent a message because the key used to encipher a message is also used to prove that a sender actually sent the message or file that was encrypted.

This section will present three types of cryptography that are currently in use — symmetric, asymmetric, and Pretty Good Privacy (PGP). It will then look at two topics related to cryptography — digital signatures and hashes.

Symmetric Cryptography

Symmetric key cryptography — also called "shared secret key" or "secret key" cryptography — uses the same key to both encipher and decipher a message or data. Symmetric key ciphers are either **block ciphers** or **stream ciphers**. A block cipher enciphers input in blocks of text using a mathematical algorithm. Stream ciphers encipher input as individual characters. The most common form of symmetric key cryptography is the Data Encryption Standard (DES), a block cipher. Other symmetric key algorithms include Advance Encryption Standard (AES), Blowfish, Twofish, and Serpent.

A practical example of symmetric cryptography is when two people — Alice and Bob — agree on an encryption method such as DES and a shared secret key. The shared key can be in the form of a password, a passphrase, or a hexadecimal string. Bob uses the key and the encryption method to encrypt a message to Alice. Alice uses the same key to decrypt the message (Figure 13).

The advantage of symmetric cryptography is that there are some fast encryption and decryption algorithms. Because the speed of a method varies with the length of the key, faster algorithms allow the use of larger key values. Larger key values make it harder to guess the key value and break the code by brute force. One disadvantage is that you have to share the key before

Symmetric Cryptosystems

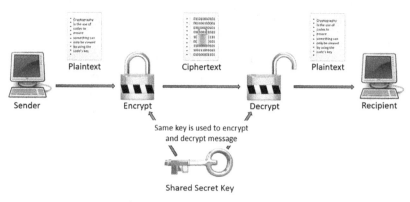

Plaintext → Ciphertext → Plaintext

Sender — Encrypt — Decrypt — Recipient

Same key is used to encrypt
and decrypt message

Shared Secret Key

Figure 13. Symmetric cryptography uses the same key to encrypt and decrypt.

you need it. This can be difficult to do securely. Another disadvantage is that in a big organization, you need a lot of keys because a separate key is required for each set of individuals who wish to encrypt messages. To have a separate key for each pair of people within a group of 100 individuals, for example, you need 4950 different keys.

Asymmetric Cryptography

Asymmetric key cryptography — also known as public key cryptography — uses a **public key** and a **private key**. These keys are created at the same time, and neither key can be mathematically derived from the other. Data encrypted with the public key can only be decrypted with the private key. Data encrypted with the private key can only be decrypted with the public key. The private key is held and kept secret by the owner of the key pair while the public key is widely published or shared with everyone you want to communicate with privately.

A practical example of asymmetric cryptography is when one person — Alice — generates a key value, usually a number or pair of related numbers, and makes it public by sharing it with Bob, Ted, Carol, and anyone else who wants it. Alice then uses this public key and some additional information to determine a second key — her private key. Alice keeps her private key and the additional information she used to construct it — as you would expect — private. Nobody has access to that key except for Alice. Anyone who has Alice's public key — Bob, for example—can use her public key to encipher and send a message to Alice. Alice can use her private key to decrypt the message. No one else can decipher the information in that message without Alice's private key or the information used to construct it (Figure 14).

The advantage of asymmetric cryptography is that it provides increased security and convenience. Private keys never need to transmitted or revealed to anyone. Only one key is

Asymmetric Cryptosystems

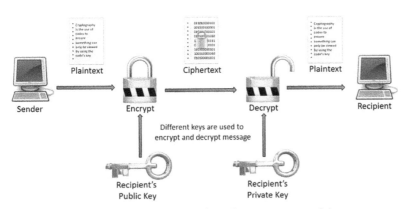

Figure 14. Asymmetric cryptosystems use two different keys to encrypt and decrypt.

needed for each recipient. The keys can provide a method for digital signatures. The disadvantage is that it is slower. There are popular secret-key encryption methods that are significantly faster than any currently available public-key encryption methods.

PGP

Pretty Good Privacy (PGP) is a computer program that provides cryptographic privacy and authentication for data communication. It's regularly used for signing, encrypting, and decrypting texts, emails, files, directories, and whole disk partitions. At its core, PGP is a hybrid cryptography system that combines features of both symmetric and asymmetric cryptography.

To encipher a data file, it creates an asymmetric key pair — a public key and a private key — and then compresses the plain-text data file to speed up encryption. PGP then creates a symmetric session key — a secret key — and encrypts the file with that session key. The session key itself is then encrypted with the public key. To decipher the file, PGP first deciphers the session key with the private key belonging to the asymmetric key pair. It then deciphers the data file with the now-decrypted session key and decompresses the data file (Figure 15).

The combination of the two encryption methods combines the convenience of public key cryptography with the speed of conventional encryption. Conventional cryptography is about 1000 times faster than public key cryptography. Public key cryptography has the benefit of providing a solution to key distribution and data transmission issues. When these methods are used together, performance and key distribution improve without sacrificing security.

PGP Cryptosystems

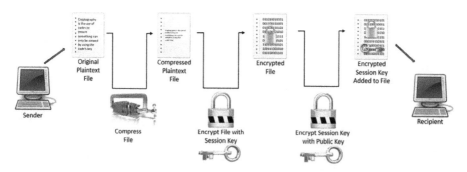

Figure 15. PGP cryptosystems use a combination of symmetric and asymmetric cryptography.

Digital Signatures

A **digital signature** is a cryptographic technique used to validate the authenticity and integrity of a message or document. Digital signatures — like handwritten signatures — are unique to each signer. They follow a specific protocol, public key infrastructure (PKI), that uses asymmetric cryptography to create a key pair. One key is public, and the other key is private. To create a digital signature, signing software creates a one-way hash or digest of the message. The private key is then used to encrypt the hash along with other information such as the hashing algorithm.

A **hash function** takes a string of characters of any length — a document or message, for example — and returns a hash or digest of that information. The ideal hash function can easily calculate a hash sum for any given input or data but make it computationally impossible to reverse engineer a hash to recreate the original text. Even changing one character in the message will result in a different hash (Figure 16).

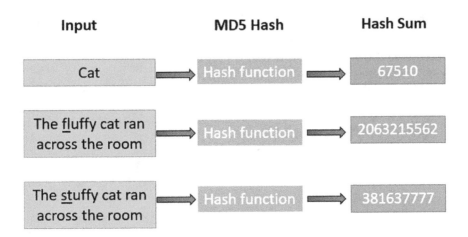

Input	MD5 Hash	Hash Sum
Cat	Hash function	67510
The fluffy cat ran across the room	Hash function	2063215562
The stuffy cat ran across the room	Hash function	381637777

Figure 16. Actual hash sums using MD5 hashing algorithm. Any change in the input text results in a different hash sum.

To see how this works in practice, let's look at how Alice will create a digital signature for her message to Bob.

First, Alice applies a publicly known hash function to a document that she wishes to sign. This hash function produces a digest of the document — usually a number. Alice then uses her private key to encipher the digest. She can then send the document with the encrypted digest to Bob, and he will be able to make sure that the message really is from Alice and that it hasn't been tampered with (Figure 17).

Sender Alice

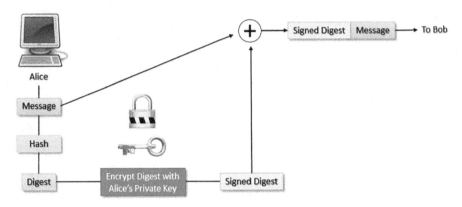

Figure 17. Signing a document with a digital signature.

Next, Bob uses Alice's public key to decipher the digest that Alice enciphered with her private key. Bob applies the hash function to the document to obtain the digest directly. Bob compares these two values for the digest. If they match, it proves that Alice signed the document and that no one else has altered it (Figure 18).

Receiver Bob

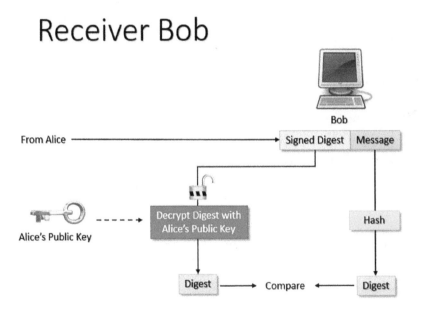

Figure 18. Using a digital signature to verify a document. If both digests are the same, the integrity is confirmed.

Chapter 9
Computer Ethics

Computer ethics is a branch of practical philosophy that's concerned with how computing professionals should make decisions regarding their professional and social conduct. Margaret Anne Pierce, a professor in the Department of Mathematics and Computers at Georgia Southern University, has categorized these ethical decisions into three primary influences:

- an individual's own personal code
- any informal code of ethical conduct that exists in the workplace
- exposure to formal codes of ethics

This chapter will help you to develop a suitable code of ethics for your own use of computers. It begins with some of the chief ethical concerns for modern computer users, including piracy, intellectual property, hacking, and privacy. Then it looks more closely at how several professional organizations have designed formal codes of ethics for computing. This will provide you with ideas for developing your personal code of ethics.

1. Intellectual Property Rights

Intellectual property is a term for creations of the intellect claimed by designated owners under law. Some common types of intellectual property rights are trademarks, copyrights, patents, industrial design rights, and — in some jurisdictions — trade secrets. These rights are for works in music, literature, film, and other artistic works; discoveries and inventions; and words, phrases, symbols, and designs that are an integral part of a business.

Figure 1.

A **patent** is a form of right granted by the government to an inventor, giving the owner the right to exclude others from making, using, selling, offering to sell, or importing an invention for a limited period of time in exchange for the public disclosure of the invention. An invention is a solution to a specific technological problem, and it may be a product or a process. It generally has to fulfill three main requirements — it has to be new, it cannot be obvious, and it must have an industrial application.

Figure 2. Patent symbol.

A **copyright** gives the creator of an original work exclusive rights to publish and earn income from it for a limited time. Copyright

Figure 3. Copyright symbol.

Figure 4. Intellectual property is protected.

may apply to a wide range of creative, intellectual, or artistic forms that have been set into some tangled form — even handwritten on a napkin. However, copyright does not protect ideas or information themselves. It only protects the form or manner by which they are expressed.

An **industrial design right**, sometimes called simply "design right," protects the visual design of objects that are not purely utilitarian. An industrial design consists of the creation of a shape, configuration or composition of pattern or color, or combination of pattern and color in three-dimensional form, and containing aesthetic value. An industrial design can be a two- or three-dimensional pattern used to produce a product, industrial commodity, or handicraft.

A **trademark** is a recognizable sign, design, or expression that distinguishes products or services of one particular business or person from the similar products or services of others. **Trade dress** is a legal term of art that generally refers to characteristics of the appearance of a product or its packaging, or even the design of a building, that signify the source of the product to consumers. A **trade secret** is a formula, practice, process, design, instrument, pattern, or compilation of information that is not generally known or easily figured out independently and that a business can use to obtain an economic advantage over competitors or customers.

The stated objective of most intellectual property law, with the exception of trademark law, is to "promote progress." By exchanging limited exclusive rights for disclosure of inventions and creative works, society and the patentee or copyright owner mutually benefit. Society gains the free use of that intellectual property after a set time. Inventors and authors have a financial incentive to create and disclose their work.

2. Intellectual Property Infringement

Violation of intellectual property rights is called "infringement" with respect to patents, copyright, and trademarks and "misappropriation" with respect to trade secrets. It may be a breach of civil law or criminal law, depending on the type of intellectual property involved, the jurisdiction, and the nature of the action. According to *The Journal of Criminal Law and Criminology*[1], as of 2011, trade in counterfeit versions of copyrighted and trademarked works was a 600-billion-dollar industry worldwide and accounted for five to seven percent of all global trade.

[1]Miriam Bitton, "Rethinking the Anti-Counterfeiting Trade Agreement's Criminal Copyright Enforcement Measures," The Journal Of Criminal Law & Criminology 102, no. 1 (2012): 67-117.

The terms "piracy" and "theft" are often associated with intellectual property infringement. The original meaning of "piracy" is "robbery or illegal violence at sea," but now the term is also used for acts of copyright infringement. "Theft" emphasizes the potential commercial harm of infringement to copyright holders, but copyright is a type of *intellectual* property, and robbery or theft are offenses related only to tangible property. Not all copyright infringement results in commercial loss, and the U.S. Supreme Court ruled in 1985 that infringement does not easily equate with theft.

Figure 5. Piracy is copyright infringement.

Organizations disagree about the economic impact of copyright infringement. The United States Government Accountability Office (GAO) clarified in 2010 that "estimating the economic impact of IP [intellectual property] infringements is extremely difficult, and assumptions must be used due to the absence of data," while "it is difficult, if not impossible, to quantify the net effect of counterfeiting and piracy on the economy as a whole."[2] In spite of this difficulty, many industry organizations and newspapers have attempted to quantity the financial cost of piracy.

Figure 6. United States Government Accountability Office logo.

In 2008, the Motion Picture Association of America (MPAA) reported that its six major member companies lost 6.1 billion dollars to piracy. A 2009 *Los Angeles Daily News* article then cited a loss figure of "roughly $20 billion a year" for Hollywood studios[3]. According to a 2013 *Wall Street Journal* article, industry estimates in the United States range between 6.1 billion and 18.5 billion dollars per year[4]. A May 2014 *Guardian* article cited an annual loss of 20.5 billion dollars for the movie industry[5].

Figure 7. Motion Picture Association of America logo.

In its 2011 report conducted in partnership with International Data Corporation and Ipsos Public Affairs, the Business Software Alliance (BSA), an anti-piracy organization, reported: "Over half of the world's personal computer users — 57 percent — admit to pirating software." The ninth annual BSA Global Software Piracy Study claims that the "commercial value of this shadow market of pirated software" was worth 63.4 billion dollars in 2011[6].

[2]US Government Accountability Office, "Intellectual Property: Observations on Efforts to Quantify the Economic Effects of Counterfeit and Pirated Goods," April 2010, http://www.gao.gov/assets/310/303057.pdf.
[3]Bob Strauss, "Film Piracy Heads North of Border," Los Angeles Daily News, April 7, 2009, http://www.dailynews.com/20090407/film-piracy-heads-north-of-border.
[4]Carl Bialik, "Putting a Price Tag on Film Piracy," Wall Street Journal, April 5, 2013, http://blogs.wsj.com/numbers/putting-a-price-tag-on-film-piracy-1228/.
[5]Samuel Gibbs, "Piracy Study Shows Illegal Downloaders More Likely to Pay for Films than Music," The Guardian, May 6, 2014, https://www.theguardian.com/technology/2014/may/06/piracy-film-music-study-pay-illegal-download-damage.
[6]Business Software Alliance, Fifth Annual BSA and IDC Global Software Piracy Study, 2007, http://globalstudy.bsa.org/2007/studies/2007_global_piracy_study.pdf.

In 2007, the Institute for Policy Innovation (IPI) reported that music piracy took 12.5 billion dollars from the U.S. economy. According to the study, musicians and those involved in the recording industry are not the only ones who experience losses attributed to music piracy. Retailers have lost over a billion dollars, while piracy has resulted in 46,000 fewer production-level jobs and almost 25,000 fewer retail jobs. The U.S. government was also reported to suffer from music piracy, losing $422 million in tax revenue.

A 2013 report released by the European Commission Joint Research Centre, however, suggests that illegal music downloads have almost no effect on the number of legal music downloads. The study analyzed the behavior of 16,000 European music consumers and found that although music piracy negatively affects offline music sales, illegal music downloads had a positive effect on legal online music purchases. Without illegal downloading, legal purchases were about two percent lower.

The study has received criticism, particularly from the International Federation of the Phonographic Industry. One argument against the research is that many music consumers only download music illegally. The IFPI also points out that music piracy affects not only online music sales but also multiple facets of the music industry that are not addressed in the study.

In spite of disagreement over the actual economic impact of copyright infringement, it's still clear that the act of piracy is common in the United States — and not just with commercial products like music albums or software but with photographs, essays, and other works that are copied and shared with others without the proper permissions.

Computers make downloading and copying files — such as music, movies, and software — incredibly easy. Because it's so easy to download and copy content found on the Internet, and because your computer won't stop you from doing so, it may appear that this is acceptable behavior. However, downloading or copying music, movies, or software without compensating their creators is a violation of their intellectual property rights, is unethical, and in some cases, is a violation of law.

Hacking

Hacking is the act of seeking and exploiting weaknesses in a computer system or computer network. Hackers may be motivated by a multitude of reasons, such as profit, protest, challenge, enjoyment, or evaluation of a system's weaknesses in order to strengthen them. In most cases, hacking is also illegal. The following fallacies are examples of the excuses users make to justify their piracy or hacking. Here we show why those justifications simply do not stand up to close scrutiny.

The No Harm Was Done Fallacy: Some hackers believe that it is okay to hack into a system as long as no damage is done to any files and nothing is taken. However, having a vulnerability exploited without permission — whether damage is done or not — is still a breach of privacy. The resources and money expended on closing the exploited loophole can also be considered a loss caused by the intrusion.

The Computer Game Fallacy: Most computer games are designed to prevent the player from cheating. Take, for example, the tile-matching game, Mahjong, where players can't make moves that are illegal. The concept that computer games make it impossible to cheat carries over to mainstream computing in the fallacy that computers, by design, will prevent users from cheating or doing anything wrong. Some hackers believe that if others didn't want their computers or programs hacked into, they should have applied better security measures. This is plainly irresponsible, and is similar to a burglar suggesting that if victims did not want their possessions stolen, they shouldn't have left their doors unlocked.

The First Amendment Fallacy: Some people in the United States believe that writing or creating a virus program is an expression of free speech and is therefore protected under the First Amendment. Creating a piece of malicious software is not expressly illegal, but *using* that software to breach the security of a computer user, causing damage or loss of resources to that user, is both unethical and illegal and can be prosecuted under federal and state laws as cybercrime.

The Shatterproof Fallacy: Many computer users are ignorant of the fact that they can do a great deal of harm through their computer activities. These individuals believe the worst they can do is damage a few files on a computer and that this damage would have a minimal effect. However, damage to the wrong file or system can be anything but minimal, and reckless experimentation like this can cause serious damage to systems.

The Hacker's Fallacy: According to this fallacy, it is acceptable to engage in any activity using a computer as long as what you are doing is motivated by learning and your intentions are not to profit by your actions. Experimenting with technology to learn more about it is encouraged throughout this book, but willingly bypassing security measures just to learn something does not represent ethical computer use. Ethical intent doesn't change the damaging nature of acts like hacking.

"White hat" hackers, who take their name from the Western movie cliché of white hats for good guys and black hats for bad guys, are sometimes employed by organizations to test the security of their systems. The white hat hacker will attempt to breach the system, and the organization employing the hacker will learn valuable information about potential weaknesses in its security. However, it is important to keep in mind that there is a big ethical boundary between hacking someone with their own permission and hacking someone without it. The former is a job. The latter is unethical and usually illegal.

The Free Information Fallacy: Some argue that all information on the Internet should be free and obtainable by any means. However, while this may be a reasonably well-argued claim in some environments, it's still just a claim and not a fact. Until this claim becomes universally accepted, it does not give permission for taking things.

3. Computing Ethics in Context

As a computer user, you join a growing number of others users across the world. Ethical computer use is the responsibility of each user.

Most computer use in the United States happens for work, whether by students for their schoolwork or professionals in their careers. The information you share, create, and view at work is available to your workplace supervisors and sometimes your peers, and the information is typically the property of your workplace. As a result, most workplaces encourage a spirit of openness in computer use.

Workplaces also come with ethical responsibilities for workers that extend to their use of computers. Sometimes these responsibilities are transmitted through the culture of the organization. Sometimes they are defined more clearly in an employee handbook. In either case, those general guidelines help to define the ethical use of computers within that context. One common ethical expectation, for example, is that workers should not use company property for personal gain. This applies to staplers and copy paper, and it also applies to computer use.

Users are increasingly incorporating computers into the context of their personal lives, too. They use computers to entertain themselves, to gather news, to communicate with friends and family, and to date. As computer use continues to increase and broaden within this context, the need to develop personal ethics also becomes increasingly important.

On social networking sites, for example, how important is it for you to tell the truth about your name, your age, or all the things that you are or are not doing? Is it acceptable to withhold or change information about yourself in order to create a false impression to others? Is it acceptable if you are doing this to protect your privacy? These are questions that aren't easy to answer but that must still be considered.

In a personal context, however, your personal code of ethics does provide a starting point for thinking about what is acceptable for your personal use of computers to interact with others. If lying is not acceptable under your personal code of ethics, then it's probably not acceptable when it comes to your personal use of computers. If telling someone's secret is not acceptable in your personal life, then it's probably not acceptable online, either.

4. Professional Codes of Ethics

Computer ethics are a developing area of study and an ongoing subject of discussion in online forums, professional organizations, university classrooms, and academic conferences. Below are the codes of ethics developed by several professional organizations.

Association for Computing Machinery Code of Ethics

Association for Computing Machinery

Figure 8. Association for Computing Machinery logo.

The Association for Computing Machinery (ACM) is an international academic society for computing. The ACM has created a Code of Ethics for its members that should apply to everyone who uses computers7. This code includes a list reprinted here to illustrate the magnitude of our responsibility when using a computer. The Code obliges ACM members to do the following:

- contribute to society and human well-being

- avoid harm to others

- be honest and trustworthy

- be fair and take action not to discriminate

- honor property rights including copyrights and patent

- give proper credit for intellectual property

- respect the privacy of others

- honor confidentiality

Australian Computer Society Code of Professional Conduct

The Australian Computer Society (ACS) is an association for information and communications technology professionals with over 22,000 members across Australia. According to its constitution, the society's goals are "to advance professional excellence in information technology" and "to promote the development of Australian information and communications technology resources." The ACS Code of Ethics says that members must uphold and advance the honor, dignity and effectiveness of being a professional. This entails, in addition to being a good citizen and acting within the law, your conformance to the following ACS values:

- The primacy of the public interest: You will place the interests of the public above those of personal, business, or sectional interests.

- The enhancement of quality of life: You will strive to enhance the quality of life of those affected by your work.

- Honesty: You will be honest in your representation of skills, knowledge, services, and products.

7Association for Computing Machinery, Code of Ethics, October 16, 1992, https://www.acm.org/about-acm/acm-code-of-ethics-and-professional-conduct.

- Competence: You will work competently and diligently for your stakeholders.

- Professional development: You will enhance your own professional development, and that of your staff.

- Professionalism: You will enhance the integrity of the ACS and the respect of its members for each other.

The Computer Ethics Institute's Ten Commandments of Computer Ethics

The Computer Ethics Institute (CEI) is a nonprofit research, education, and public policy organization focused on the issues, dilemmas, and challenges of advancing information technology within ethical frameworks. CEI's mission is to facilitate the examination and recognition of ethical issues in the development and use of modern information technologies. The output of this discussion provides educational resources and governing rules that have been adopted by many schools, organizations, and corporations around the globe. The CEI has created what it calls "The Ten Commandments of Computer Ethics"8:

1. You shall not use a computer to harm other people.

2. You shall not interfere with other people's computer work.

3. You shall not snoop around in other people's computer files.

4. You shall not use a computer to steal.

5. You shall not use a computer to bear false witness.

6. You shall not copy or use proprietary software for which you have not paid (without permission).

7. You shall not use other people's computer resources without authorization or proper compensation.

8. You shall not appropriate other people's intellectual output.

9. You shall think about the social consequences of the program you are writing or the system you are designing.

10. You shall always use a computer in ways that ensure consideration and respect for your fellow humans.

---

[8] Computer Ethics Institute, Ten Commandments of Computer Ethics, http://computerethicsinstitute.org/publications/tencommandments.html.

The British Computer Society Code of Ethics

The British Computer Society is a professional body and a learned society representing those working in Information Technology both in the United Kingdom and internationally. Its objectives are to promote the study and application of communications technology and computing technology and to advance knowledge of education in ICT [Information and Communications Technology] for the benefit of professional practitioners and the general public[9].

Figure 9. British Computer Society logo.

Public Interest. You shall:

- have due regard for public health, privacy, security, and wellbeing of others and the environment.

- have due regard for the legitimate rights of third parties.

- conduct your professional activities without discrimination on the grounds of sex, sexual orientation, marital status, nationality, color, race, ethnic origin, religion, age or disability, or of any other condition or requirement.

- promote equal access to the benefits of IT and seek to promote the inclusion of all sectors in society wherever opportunities arise.

Professional Competence and Integrity. You shall:

- only undertake to do work or provide a service that is within your professional competence.

- not claim any level of competence that you do not possess.

- develop your professional knowledge, skills and competence on a continuing basis, maintaining awareness of technological developments, procedures, and standards that are relevant to your field.

- ensure that you have the knowledge and understanding of legislation and that you comply with such legislation, in carrying out your professional responsibilities.

- respect and value alternative viewpoints and seek, accept and offer honest criticisms of work.

- avoid injuring others, their property, reputation, or employment by false or malicious or negligent action or inaction.

- reject and will not make any offer of bribery or unethical inducement.

---

[9] British Computer Society, BCS Code of Conduct, http://www.bcs.org/upload/pdf/conduct.pdf.

Duty to Relevant Authority. You shall:

- carry out your professional responsibilities with due care and diligence in accordance with the Relevant Authority's requirements whilst exercising your professional judgment at all times.

- seek to avoid any situation that may give rise to a conflict of interest between you and your Relevant Authority.

- accept professional responsibility for your work and for the work of colleagues who are defined in a given context as working under your supervision.

- NOT disclose or authorize to be disclosed, or use for personal gain or to benefit a third party, confidential information except with the permission of your Relevant Authority, or as required by Legislation.

- NOT misrepresent or withhold information on the performance of products, systems or services (unless lawfully bound by a duty of confidentiality not to disclose such information), or take advantage of the lack of relevant knowledge or inexperience of others.

Duty to the Profession. You shall:
- accept your personal duty to uphold the reputation of the profession and not take any action which could bring the profession into disrepute.

- seek to improve professional standards through participation in their development, use and enforcement.

- uphold the reputation and good standing of BCS, the chartered institute for IT.

- act with integrity and respect in your professional relationships with all members of BCS and with members of other professions with whom you work in a professional capacity.

- notify BCS if convicted of a criminal offense or upon becoming bankrupt or disqualified as a Company Director and in each case give details of the relevant jurisdiction.

- encourage and support fellow members in their professional development.

The System Administrators' Code of Ethics

Figure 10. The League of Professional System Administrators.

The League of Professional System Administrators (LOPSA) is a nonprofit corporation with members throughout the world. Its mission is to advance the practice of system administration; to support, recognize, educate, and encourage its practitioners; and to serve the public through education and outreach on system administration issues. What follows is LOPSA's Code of Ethics[10].

We, as professional system administrators, do hereby commit ourselves to the highest standards of ethical and professional conduct, and agree to be guided by this code of ethics, and encourage every System Administrator to do the same.

- **Professionalism:** I will maintain professional conduct in the workplace, and will not allow personal feelings or beliefs to cause me to treat people unfairly or unprofessionally.

- **Personal Integrity:** I will be honest in my professional dealings, and forthcoming about my competence and the impact of my mistakes. I will seek assistance from others when required. I will avoid conflicts of interest and biases whenever possible. When my advice is sought, if I have a conflict of interest or bias, I will declare it if appropriate, and recuse myself if necessary.

- **Privacy:** I will access private information on computer systems only when it is necessary in the course of my technical duties. I will maintain and protect the confidentiality of any information to which I may have access regardless of the method by which I came into knowledge of it.

- **Laws and Policies:** I will educate myself and others on relevant laws, regulations, and policies regarding the performance of my duties.

- **Communication:** I will communicate with management, users, and colleagues about computer matters of mutual interest. I will strive to listen to and understand the needs of all parties.

- **System Integrity:** I will strive to ensure the necessary integrity, reliability, and availability of the systems for which I am responsible. I will design and maintain each system in a manner to support the purpose of the system to the organization.

- **Education:** I will continue to update and enhance my technical knowledge and other work-related skills. I will share my knowledge and experience with others.

---

[10] The League of Professional System Administrators, Code of Ethics, 2006, https://lopsa.org/CodeOfEthics.

- **Responsibility to Computing Community:** I will cooperate with the larger computing community to maintain the integrity of network and computing resources.

- **Social Responsibility:** As an informed professional, I will encourage the writing and adoption of relevant policies and laws consistent with these ethical principles.

- **Ethical Responsibility:** I will strive to build and maintain a safe, healthy, and productive workplace. I will do my best to make decisions consistent with the safety, privacy, and well-being of my community and the public, and to disclose promptly factors that might pose unexamined risks or dangers. I will accept and offer honest criticism of technical work as appropriate and will credit properly the contributions of others. I will lead by example, maintaining a high ethical standard and degree of professionalism in the performance of all my duties. I will support colleagues and co-workers in following this code of ethics.

Acknowledgments

Text Acknowledgments

Chapter 1

"Input/Output." Wikipedia. Wikipedia.org. Last modified August 3, 2016. Original material licensed under a Creative Commons CC-BY-SA 3.0 Unported License.

Computers for Beginners. Wikibooks.org. Last modified December 14, 2015. Original material licensed under a Creative Commons CC-BY-SA 3.0 Unported License.

"Data (computing)." Wikipedia. Wikipedia.org. Last modified August 8, 2016. Original material licensed under a Creative Commons CC-BY-SA 3.0 Unported License.

"Server (computing)." Wikipedia.Wikipedia.org. Last modified August 13, 2016. Original material licensed under a Creative Commons CC-BY-SA 3.0 Unported License.

"File server." Wikipedia. Wikipedia.org. Last modified March 11, 2016. Original material licensed under a Creative Commons CC-BY-SA 3.0 Unported License.

"Mainframe computer." Wikipedia. Wikipedia.org. Last modified August 6, 2016. Original material licensed under a Creative Commons CC-BY-SA 3.0 Unported License.

"Vacuum tube." Wikipedia. Wikipedia.org. Last modified August 8, 2016. Original material licensed under a Creative Commons CC-BY-SA 3.0 Unported License.

"Transistor." Wikipedia. Wikipedia.org. Last modified August 13, 2016. Original material licensed under a Creative Commons CC-BY-SA 3.0 Unported License.

"Integrated circuit." Wikipedia. Wikipedia.org. Last modified August 8, 2016. Original material licensed under a Creative Commons CC-BY-SA 3.0 Unported License.

History of Computers. Wikibooks.org. Last modified October 22, 2015. Original material licensed under a Creative Commons CC-BY-SA 3.0 Unported License.

Chapter 2

Computer Hardware. Wikibooks.org. Last modified June 28, 2016. Original material licensed under a Creative Commons CC-BY-SA 3.0 Unported License.

"Input device." *Wikipedia.* Wikipedia.org. Last modified August 9, 2016. Original material licensed under a Creative Commons CC-BY-SA 3.0 Unported License.

"Output device." *Wikipedia.* Wikipedia.org. Last modified August 11, 2016. Original material licensed under a Creative Commons CC-BY-SA 3.0 Unported License.

"Cathode ray tube." *Wikipedia.* Wikipedia.org. Last modified August 15, 2016. Original material licensed under a Creative Commons CC-BY-SA 3.0 Unported License.

"Liquid-crystal display." *Wikipedia.* Wikipedia.org. Last modified August 12, 2016. Original material licensed under a Creative Commons CC-BY-SA 3.0 Unported License.

"Optical disc drive." *Wikipedia.* Wikipedia.org. Last modified July 22, 2016. Original material licensed under a Creative Commons CC-BY-SA 3.0 Unported License.

"DVD." *Wikipedia.* Wikipedia.org. Last modified July 21, 2016. Original material licensed under a Creative Commons CC-BY-SA 3.0 Unported License.

"Blu-ray." *Wikipedia.* Wikipedia.org. Last modified August 15, 2016. Original material licensed under a Creative Commons CC-BY-SA 3.0 Unported License.

"Hard disk drive." *Wikipedia.* Wikipedia.org. Last modified August 9, 2016. Original material licensed under a Creative Commons CC-BY-SA 3.0 Unported License.

"Solid-state drive." *Wikipedia.* Wikipedia.org. Last modified August 12, 2016. Original material licensed under a Creative Commons CC-BY-SA 3.0 Unported License.

"CompactFlash." *Wikipedia.* Wikipedia.org. Last modified June 18, 2016. Original material licensed under a Creative Commons CC-BY-SA 3.0 Unported License.

"Secure Digital." *Wikipedia.* Wikipedia.org. Last modified August 8, 2016. Original material licensed under a Creative Commons CC-BY-SA 3.0 Unported License.

"USB flash drive." *Wikipedia.* Wikipedia.org. Last modified August 14, 2016. Original material licensed under a Creative Commons CC-BY-SA 3.0 Unported License.

"Printer (computing)." *Wikipedia.* Wikipedia.org. Last modified July 31, 2016. Original material licensed under a Creative Commons CC-BY-SA 3.0 Unported License.

"Radio-frequency identification." *Wikipedia.* Wikipedia.org. Last modified August 11, 2016. Original material licensed under a Creative Commons CC-BY-SA 3.0 Unported License.

"Remote control." *Wikipedia.* Wikipedia.org. Last modified August 1, 2016. Original material licensed under a Creative Commons CC-BY-SA 3.0 Unported License.

"Biometrics." *Wikipedia.* Wikipedia.org. Last modified August 10, 2016. Original material licensed under a Creative Commons CC-BY-SA 3.0 Unported License.

"Projector." *Wikipedia.* Wikipedia.org. Last modified June 22, 2016. Original material licensed under a Creative Commons CC-BY-SA 3.0 Unported License.

"Digital Light Processing." *Wikipedia.* Wikipedia.org. Last modified June 21, 2016. Original material licensed under a Creative Commons CC-BY-SA 3.0 Unported License.

"Plotter." *Wikipedia.* Wikipedia.org. Last modified May 10, 2016. Original material licensed under a Creative Commons CC-BY-SA 3.0 Unported License.

"USB." *Wikipedia.* Wikipedia.org. Last modified August 14, 2016. Original material licensed under a Creative Commons CC-BY-SA 3.0 Unported License.

"IEEE 1394." *Wikipedia.* Wikipedia.org. Last modified August 14, 2016. Original material licensed under a Creative Commons CC-BY-SA 3.0 Unported License.

"Serial ATA." *Wikipedia.* Wikipedia.org. Last modified August 2, 2016. Original material licensed under a Creative Commons CC-BY-SA 3.0 Unported License.

"SCSI." *Wikipedia.* Wikipedia.org. Last modified August 13, 2016. Original material licensed under a Creative Commons CC-BY-SA 3.0 Unported License.

"Bluetooth." *Wikipedia.* Wikipedia.org. Last modified August 15, 2016. Original material licensed under a Creative Commons CC-BY-SA 3.0 Unported License.

Chapter 3

"File Explorer." *Wikipedia.* Wikipedia.org. Last modified August 6, 2016. Original material licensed under a Creative Commons CC-BY-SA 3.0 Unported License.

Mac OS X Tiger. Wikibooks.org. Last modified September 24, 2006. Original material licensed under a Creative Commons CC-BY-SA 3.0 Unported License.

Chapter 4

"Operating system." *Wikipedia.* Wikipedia.org. Last modified August 8, 2016. Original material licensed under a Creative Commons CC-BY-SA 3.0 Unported License.

"Adobe Photoshop." *Wikipedia.* Wikipedia.org. Last modified August 14, 2016. Original material licensed under a Creative Commons CC-BY-SA 3.0 Unported License.

"Pro Tools." *Wikipedia.* Wikipedia.org. Last modified August 6, 2016. Original material licensed under a Creative Commons CC-BY-SA 3.0 Unported License.

"Garageband." *Wikipedia.* Wikipedia.org. Last modified August 2, 2016. Original material licensed under a Creative Commons CC-BY-SA 3.0 Unported License.

"Audacity (audio editor)." *Wikipedia.* Wikipedia.org. Last modified July 31, 2016. Original material licensed under a Creative Commons CC-BY-SA 3.0 Unported License.

"Antivirus software." *Wikipedia.* Wikipedia.org. Last modified August 7, 2016. Original material licensed under a Creative Commons CC-BY-SA 3.0 Unported License.

Chapter 5

"Computer network." *Wikipedia.* Wikipedia.org. Last modified August 15, 2016. Original material licensed under a Creative Commons CC-BY-SA 3.0 Unported License.

"Transaction processing system." *Wikipedia.* Wikipedia.org. Last modified June 20, 2016. Original material licensed under a Creative Commons CC-BY-SA 3.0 Unported License.

"Management information system." *Wikipedia.* Wikipedia.org. Last modified August 11, 2016. Original material licensed under a Creative Commons CC-BY-SA 3.0 Unported License.

"Decision support system." *Wikipedia.* Wikipedia.org. Last modified May 29, 2016. Original material licensed under a Creative Commons CC-BY-SA 3.0 Unported License.

"Expert system." *Wikipedia.* Wikipedia.org. Last modified August 15, 2016. Original material licensed under a Creative Commons CC-BY-SA 3.0 Unported License.

"Surface web." *Wikipedia.* Wikipedia.org. Last modified March 12, 2016. Original material licensed under a Creative Commons CC-BY-SA 3.0 Unported License.

"Deep web." *Wikipedia.* Wikipedia.org. Last modified August 12, 2016. Original material licensed under a Creative Commons CC-BY-SA 3.0 Unported License.

Chapter 6

"Email." *Wikipedia.* Wikipedia.org. Last modified August 15, 2016. Original material licensed under a Creative Commons CC-BY-SA 3.0 Unported License.

"WebRTC." *Wikipedia.* Wikipedia.org. Last modified August 3, 2016. Original material licensed under a Creative Commons CC-BY-SA 3.0 Unported License.

"Telepresence." *Wikipedia.* Wikipedia.org. Last modified June 25, 2016. Original material licensed under a Creative Commons CC-BY-SA 3.0 Unported License.

"Social media." *Wikipedia.* Wikipedia.org. Last modified August 15, 2016. Original material licensed under a Creative Commons CC-BY-SA 3.0 Unported License.

"Leading social networks worldwide as of April 2016, ranked by number of active users (in millions)." *Statista.* Statista.com. Accessed June 3, 2016. Used with permission. http://www.statista.com/statistics/272014/global-social-networks-ranked-by-number-of-users/

"Active social network penetration in selected countries as of January 2016." Statista. Statista.com. Accessed June 3, 2016. Used with permission (http://www.statista.com/statistics/282846/regular-social-networking-usage-penetration-worldwide-by-country/).

"Etiquette in technology." *Wikipedia.* Wikipedia.org. Last modified August 10, 2016. Original material licensed under a Creative Commons CC-BY-SA 3.0 Unported License.

Chapter 7

"Internet." *Wikipedia.* Wikipedia.org. Last modified August 15, 2016. Original material licensed under a Creative Commons CC-BY-SA 3.0 Unported License.

"ARPANET." *Wikipedia.* Wikipedia.org. Last modified July 24, 2016. Original material licensed under a Creative Commons CC-BY-SA 3.0 Unported License.

"Web browser." *Wikipedia.* Wikipedia.org. Last modified August 15, 2016. Original material licensed under a Creative Commons CC-BY-SA 3.0 Unported License.

"Uniform Resource Identifier." *Wikipedia.* Wikipedia.org. Last modified August 10, 2016. Original material licensed under a Creative Commons CC-BY-SA 3.0 Unported License.

"Hyperlink." *Wikipedia.* Wikipedia.org. Last modified August 6, 2016. Original material licensed under a Creative Commons CC-BY-SA 3.0 Unported License.

"Plug-in (computing)." *Wikipedia.* Wikipedia.org. Last modified July 30, 2016. Original material licensed under a Creative Commons CC-BY-SA 3.0 Unported License.

"World Wide Web." *Wikipedia.* Wikipedia.org. Last modified August 15, 2016. Original material licensed under a Creative Commons CC-BY-SA 3.0 Unported License.

"Domain Name System." *Wikipedia.* Wikipedia.org. Last modified August 14, 2016. Original material licensed under a Creative Commons CC-BY-SA 3.0 Unported License.

"Web search engine." *Wikipedia.* Wikipedia.org. Last modified August 12, 2016. Original material licensed under a Creative Commons CC-BY-SA 3.0 Unported License.

"Surface web." *Wikipedia.* Wikipedia.org. Last modified March 12, 2016. Original material licensed under a Creative Commons CC-BY-SA 3.0 Unported License.

"Deep web." *Wikipedia.* Wikipedia.org. Last modified August 12, 2016. Original material licensed under a Creative Commons CC-BY-SA 3.0 Unported License.

"Dark web." *Wikipedia.* Wikipedia.org. Last modified August 6, 2016. Original material licensed under a Creative Commons CC-BY-SA 3.0 Unported License.

Chapter 8

Basic Computer Security. Wikibooks.org. Last modified July 23, 2016. Original material licensed under a Creative Commons CC-BY-SA 3.0 Unported License.

"Computer security." *Wikipedia.* Wikipedia.org. Last modified August 12, 2016. Original material licensed under a Creative Commons CC-BY-SA 3.0 Unported License.

"Password strength." *Wikipedia.* Wikipedia.org. Last modified August 5, 2016. Original material licensed under a Creative Commons CC-BY-SA 3.0 Unported License.

"Internet security." *Wikipedia.* Wikipedia.org. Last modified August 5, 2016. Original material licensed under a Creative Commons CC-BY-SA 3.0 Unported License.

"Network security." *Wikipedia.* Wikipedia.org. Last modified August 3, 2016. Original material licensed under a Creative Commons CC-BY-SA 3.0 Unported License.

"Cryptography." *Wikipedia.* Wikipedia.org. Last modified July 25, 2016. Original material licensed under a Creative Commons CC-BY-SA 3.0 Unported License.

"Information security." *Wikipedia.* Wikipedia.org. Last modified August 9, 2016. Original material licensed under a Creative Commons CC-BY-SA 3.0 Unported License.

"Transport Layer Security." *Wikipedia.* Wikipedia. org. Last modified August 10, 2016. Original material licensed under a Creative Commons CC-BY-SA 3.0 Unported License.

"Mobile security." *Wikipedia.* Wikipedia.org. Last modified August 11, 2016. Original material licensed under a Creative Commons CC-BY-SA 3.0 Unported License.

Official US Government Information about the Global Positioning System (GPS) and Related Topics. GPS.gov. All rights granted under Public Domain because this website and its content is a work of the United States government.

"Cloud computing." *Wikipedia.* Wikipedia.org. Last modified August 14, 2016. Original material licensed under a Creative Commons CC-BY-SA 3.0 Unported License.

"Cloud computing security." *Wikipedia.* Wikipedia. org. Last modified August 11, 2016. Original material licensed under a Creative Commons CC-BY-SA 3.0 Unported License.

Chapter 9

"Copyright infringement." Wikipedia. Wikipedia.org. Last modified August 5, 2016. Original material licensed under a Creative Commons CC-BY-SA 3.0 Unported License.

"Intellectual property." Wikipedia. Wikipedia.org. Last modified August 5, 2016. Original material licensed under a Creative Commons CC-BY-SA 3.0 Unported License.

"Intellectual rights." Wikipedia. Wikipedia.org. Last modified July 6, 2016. Original material licensed under a Creative Commons CC-BY-SA 3.0 Unported License.

"Computer Ethics." Wikipedia.org. Last modified June 4, 2016. Original material licensed under a Creative Commons CC-BY-SA 3.0 Unported License.

Image Acknowledgments

Chapter 1

Chapter 2

Figure 2.1. "Apple-wireless-keyboard-aluminum-2007" by Roadmr is licensed under CC BY-SA 4.0 (https://commons.wikimedia.org/wiki/File:Apple-wireless-keyboard-aluminum-2007.jpg).

Figure 2.2. "Assorted computer mice - MfK Bern" by Sandstein is licensed under CC BY-SA 3.0 (https://commons.wikimedia.org/wiki/File:Assorted_computer_mice_-_MfK_Bern.jpg).

Figure 2.3. "Dell XPS 15z" by GillyBerlin is licensed under CC BY 2.0 (https://www.flickr.com/photos/gillyberlin/6342833763).

Figure 2.4. "Nikon COOLPIX P7700 front" by Thilo Parg is licensed under CC BY-SA 3.0 (https://commons.wikimedia.org/wiki/File:Nikon_COOLPIX_P7700_front.JPG).

Figure 2.5. "Nikon D3100" by Nikon Polska is licensed under CC BY 2.0 (https://commons.wikimedia.org/wiki/File:Nikon_D3100.jpg).

Figure 2.6. "Webcam" by Aksa2011 is licensed under CC0 Public Domain (https://pixabay.com/en/camera-webcam-computer-internet-1219748/).

Figure 2.7. "Canon CanoScan LiDE40" by Qurren is licensed under CC BY-SA 3.0 (https://commons.wikimedia.org/wiki/File:Canon_CanoScan_LiDE40.jpg).

Figure 2.8. "Image of barcode reader" by 条形码阅读器 is licensed under CC0 Public Domain (http://www.publicdomainpictures.net/view-image.php?image=73863&picture=&jazyk=CN).

Figure 2.9. "RFID Chip 004" by Maschinenjunge is licensed under CC BY-SA 3.0 (https://commons.wikimedia.org/wiki/File:RFID_Chip_004.JPG).

Figure 2.10. "Thinkpad docking station with T61 laptop" by Ximeg is licensed under CC BY-SA 3.0 (https://commons.wikimedia.org/wiki/File:Thinkpad_docking_station_with_T61_laptop.JPG).

Figure 2.11. "Microphone gooseneck" by Zzubnik is licensed under CC0 Public Domain (https://commons.wikimedia.org/wiki/File:Microphone_gooseneck.jpg).

Figure 2.12. "Wacom Intuos pen & touch M" by Medvedev is licensed under CC BY-SA 3.0 (https://commons.wikimedia.org/wiki/File:Wacom_Intuos_pen_%26_touch_M.jpg).

Figure 2.13. "Aldea Digital 2013 01" by ProtoplasmaKid is licensed under CC BY-SA 3.0 (https://commons.wikimedia.org/wiki/File:Aldea_Digital_2013_01.jpg).

Figure 2.14. "Light Man Hand Pen" by Karolina Grabowska is licensed under CC0 Public Domain (https://www.pexels.com/photo/hand-using-stylus-pen-for-touching-the-digital-tablet-screen-6336/).

Figure 2.15. "Remote control" by nuzree is licensed under CC0 Public Domain (https://pixabay.com/en/remote-control-tv-television-remote-205828/).

Figure 2.16. "Game Controllers" by Ted Mielczarek is licensed under CC0 Public Domain (https://www.flickr.com/photos/49243838@N00/11241518385).

Figure 2.17. "Fingerprint scanner identification" by Rachmaninoff is licensed under CC BY-SA 3.0 (https://commons.wikimedia.org/wiki/File:Fingerprint_scanner_identification.jpg).

Figure 2.18. "ASUS CD-ROM CD-S520-A4 20080821" by Asim18 is licensed under CC BY-SA 3.0 (https://commons.wikimedia.org/wiki/File:ASUS_CD-ROM_CD-S520-A4_20080821.jpg).

Figure 2.19. "WD 1TB 3.5 inch Internal Hard Drive - Caviar Blue" by Shakib Saifi is licensed under CC BY 2.0 (https://www.flickr.com/photos/126850594@N06/14714708258).

Figure 2.20. "Portable Hard Disk 1TB Western Digital" by Harke is licensed under CC BY-SA 3.0 (https://commons.wikimedia.org/wiki/File:Portable_Hard_Disk_1TB_Western_Digital.jpg).

Figure 2.21. "Intel X25-M Solid-State Drive" by Intel Free Press is licensed under CC BY 2.0 (https://commons.wikimedia.org/wiki/File:Intel_X25-M_Solid-State_Drive.jpg).

Figure 2.22. "SANDISK Extreme CompactFlash card 16 GB 60 MBs - 2015 - 001" by Thesupermat is licensed under CC BY-SA 4.0 (https://commons.wikimedia.org/wiki/File:SANDISK_Extreme_CompactFlash_card_16_GB_60_MBs_-_2015_-_001.jpg).

Figure 2.23. "Micro Sd Card" by Petr Kratochvil is licensed under CC0 Public Domain (http://www.publicdomainpictures.net/view-image.php?image=25303).

Chapter 3

Chapter 4

Figure 4.1. "Desktop Ubuntu 13 10" by Funkruf is licensed under CC BY-SA 3.0 (https://commons.wikimedia.org/wiki/File:Desktop_Ubuntu_13_10.png).

Figure 4.2. "FreeDOS Beta 9 pre-release5 (command line interface) on Bochs sshot20040912" by (of program) Jim Hall and others, (of screenshot) Krzysztof Burghardt, is licensed under Public Domain (https://commons.wikimedia.org/wiki/File:FreeDOS_Beta_9_pre-release5_(command_line_interface)_on_Bochs_sshot20040912.png).

Figure 4.3. "Smartphone" by Pexels is licensed under CC0 Public Domain (https://pixabay.com/en/smartphone-technology-mockup-apps-1283938/).

Figure 4.4. "Audi TT 2014 (13558812864)" by Robert Basic is licensed under CC BY-SA 2.0 (https://commons.wikimedia.org/wiki/File:Audi_TT_2014_(13558812864).jpg).

Figure 4.5. "Various applications" by Cierra Maher is a product of work by Chemeketa Press. All rights reserved.

Chapter 5

Figure 5.1. "Networking" by Charles Rondeau is licensed under CC0 Public Domain (http://www.publicdomainpictures.net/view-image.php?image=78371&picture=network).

Figure 5.2. "SAN " by Candace Johnson is a product of work by Chemeketa Press. All rights reserved.

Figure 5.3. "VPN" by Candace Johnson is a product of work by Chemeketa Press. All rights reserved.

Figure 5.4. "Coaxial cable cut" by FDominec is licensed under CC BY-SA 3.0 (https://commons.wikimedia.org/wiki/File:Coaxial_cable_cut.jpg).

Figure 5.5. "FTP cable3" by Baran Ivo is licensed under CC0 Public Domain (https://commons.wikimedia.org/wiki/File:FTP_cable3.jpg).

Figure 5.6. "Fiber-optic communications" by http://www.ictas.vt.edu is licensed under CC BY-SA 4.0 (https://commons.wikimedia.org/wiki/file:%D9%85%D8%AE%D8%A7%D8%A8%D8%B1%D8%A7%D8%AA_%D9%81%DB%8C%D8%A8%D8%B1_%D9%86%D9%88%D8%B1%DB%8C.jpg).

Figure 5.7. "Wireless technology" by Candace Johnson is a product of work by Chemeketa Press. All rights reserved.

Figure 5.8. "Network card" by Helix84 is licensed under CC BY-SA 3.0 (https://commons.wikimedia.org/wiki/File:Network_card.jpg).

Figure 5.9. "USB Dongle WiFi stick on computer" by Santeri Viinamäki is licensed under CC BY-SA 3.0 (https://commons.wikimedia.org/wiki/File:USB_Dongle_WiFi_stick_on_computer.jpg).

Figure 5.10. "2550T-PWR-Front" by Geek2003 is licensed under CC BY-SA 4.0 (https://commons.wikimedia.org/wiki/File:2550T-PWR-Front.jpg).

Figure 5.11. "Linksys-Wireless-G-Router" by Evan-Amos is licensed under CC0 Public Domain (https://commons.wikimedia.org/wiki/File:Linksys-Wireless-G-Router.jpg).

Figure 5.12. "Linksys ADSL Modem AM300" by Feureau is licensed under CC BY-SA 3.0 (https://commons.wikimedia.org/wiki/File:Linksys_ADSL_Modem_AM300.jpg).

Figure 5.13. "Firewall" by Bruno Pedrozo is licensed under CC BY-SA 3.0 (https://en.wikipedia.org/wiki/Firewall_(computing)#/media/File:Firewall.png).

Figure 5.14. "NetworkTopologies" by Maksim is a derivative of work by Malyszkz, and is licensed under CC0 Public Domain (https://commons.wikimedia.org/wiki/File:NetworkTopologies.svg).

Figure 5.15. "Extranet" by Emily Evans is a product of work by Chemeketa Press. All rights reserved.

Figure 5.16. "Credit-cards" by Lotus Head is licensed under CC BY-SA 3.0 (https://commons.wikimedia.org/wiki/File:Credit-cards.jpg).

Figure 5.17. "Database" by Faith Martinmaas is a product of work by Chemeketa Press. All rights reserved.

Figure 5.18. "Artificial-intelligence-elon-musk-hawking" by A Health Blog/Flickr is licensed under CC BY-SA 2.0 (https://www.flickr.com/photos/healthblog/8384110298/in/photostream/).

Figure 5.19. "TCP/IP Wifi stack?" by Kristi Etzel is a product of work by Chemeketa Press. All rights reserved.

Figure 5.20. "Network services (WWW, Email, printing, file sharing)" by Candace Johnson is a product of work by Chemeketa Press. All rights reserved.

Figure 5.21. "E2EE " by Emily Evans is a product of work by Chemeketa Press. All rights reserved.

Chapter 6

Figure 6.1. "Imagen - e-mail Marketing" by RaHuL Rodriguez is licensed under CC BY-SA 2.0 (https://www.flickr.com/photos/rahulrodriguez/9026700946).

Figure 6.2. "Botnet (spamming)" by Tom-b/Wikimedia Commons is licensed under CC BY-SA 3.0 (https://commons.wikimedia.org/wiki/File:Botnet.svg).

Figure 6.3. "Email Bombing" by Emily Evans is a product of work by Chemeketa Press. All rights reserved.

Figure 6.4. "Phishing" by Edwind Richzendy Contreras Soto is licensed under CC BY-SA 2.0 (https://www.flickr.com/photos/35484468@N07/4894714911).

Figure 6.5. "Privacy concerns" by Emily Evans is a product of work by Chemeketa Press. All rights reserved.

Figure 6.6. "Teliris VL Modular" by Fuelrefuel/Wikimedia commons is licensed under CC BY-SA 3.0 (https://commons.wikimedia.org/wiki/File:Teliris_VL_Modular.JPG).

Figure 6.7. "Shadow Hand Bulb large" by Richard Greenhill and Hugo Elias (myself) of the Shadow Robot Company is licensed under CC BY-SA 3.0 (https://commons.wikimedia.org/wiki/File:Shadow_Hand_Bulb_large.jpg).

Figure 6.8. "Virtual Reality OR" by Cornell Urology is licensed under CC BY-SA 3.0 (https://en.wikipedia.org/wiki/File:Virtual_Reality_OR.jpg).

Figure 6.9. "NASA Mars Rover" by NASA/JPL/Cornell University, Maas Digital LLC is licensed under CC0 Public Domain (https://commons.wikimedia.org/wiki/File:NASA_Mars_Rover.jpg).

Figure 6.10. "Suitable Technologies Beam telepresence robot" by Intel Free Press is licensed under CC BY-SA 2.0 (https://commons.wikimedia.org/wiki/File:Suitable_Technologies_Beam_telepresence_robot.jpg).

Figure 6.11. "Automotive Social Media Marketing Infographics" by DigitalRalph is licensed under CC BY 2.0 (https://www.flickr.com/photos/ralphpaglia/5460685914).

Figure 6.12. "Top Social Network timeline" by Ronald Cox IV is a product of work by Chemeketa Press. All rights reserved.

Figure 6.13. "Positive Effects of Social Media" by Emily Evans is a product of work by Chemeketa Press. All rights reserved.

Figure 6.14. "The Day We Fight Back - banner (privacy)" by Alec Perkins is licensed under CC BY 4.0 (https://commons.wikimedia.org/wiki/File:The_Day_We_Fight_Back_-_banner.jpg).

Figure 6.15. "Developed and developing countries" by Sbw01f/Wikimedia commons is licensed under CC BY-SA 3.0 (https://commons.wikimedia.org/wiki/File:Developed_and_developing_countries.PNG).

Figure 6.16. "InternetPenetrationWorldMap" by Jeff Ogden (W163)/Wikimedia commons is licensed under CC BY-SA 3.0 (https://commons.wikimedia.org/wiki/File:InternetPenetrationWorldMap.svg).

Figure 6.17. "Netiquette" by Faith Martinmaas is a product of work by Chemeketa Press. All rights reserved.

Figure 6.18. "Cross-posting" by Kristi Etzel is a product of work by Chemeketa Press. All rights reserved.

Figure 6.19. "Email Signature - July 2010" by mjmonty is licensed under CC BY 2.0 (https://www.flickr.com/photos/mjmonty/4779934613).

Figure 6.20. "Emoticon Smile Face" by IkamusumeFan/Wikimedia commons is licensed under CC0 Public Domain (https://commons.wikimedia.org/wiki/File:Emoticon_Smile_Face.svg).

Figure 6.21. "Emojis" by Unicode are copyrighted content and may not be used without additional Permission by Unicode (http://www.unicode.org/copyright.html).

Chapter 7

Chapter 8

Figure 8.1. "Cyber Security - Cyber Crime" by www.bluecoat.com is licensed under CC BY-SA 2.0 (https://www.flickr.com/photos/111692634@N04/18709586962).

Figure 8.2. "Types-of-malware" by Gelibnuira/Wikimedia commons is licensed under CC BY-SA 4.0 (https://commons.wikimedia.org/wiki/File:Types-of-malware.png).

Figure 8.3. "Passwords" by Kristi Etzel is a product of work by Chemeketa Press. All rights reserved.

Figure 8.4. "Windows Update" by Stephen Edgar is licensed under CC BY-SA 2.0 (https://www.flickr.com/photos/netweb/163468567).

Figure 8.5. "Firewalls" by Candace Johnson is a product of work by Chemeketa Press. All rights reserved.

Figure 8.6. "Security software" by Avast is used under Fair Use guidelines (https://www.avast.com/media-materials).

Figure 8.7. "GPS" by DariuszSankowski is licensed under CC0 Public Domain (https://pixabay.com/en/navigation-car-drive-road-gps-1048294/).

Figure 8.8. Created using clipart © 2017 by Presenter Media and the Open Source Initiative. Used by permission.

Figure 8.9. "Devices in the Cloud - Technology" by Blue Coat Photos www.bluecoat.com is licensed

under CC BY-SA 2.0 (https://www.flickr.com/photos/111692634@N04/16203260320).

Figure 8.10. "Backing up your data" by Faith Martinmaas is a product of work by Chemeketa Press. All rights reserved.

Figure 8.11. "E-commerce" by Garfield Anderssen is licensed under CC BY 2.0 (https://www.flickr.com/photos/78855484@N03/7223384344).

Figure 8.12. "Orange blue public key cryptography en" by Bananenfalter is licensed under CC0 Public Domain (https://commons.wikimedia.org/wiki/File:Orange_blue_public_key_cryptography_en.svg).

Figure 8.13. Created using clipart © 2017 by Presenter Media and the Open Source Initiative. Used by permission.

Figure 8.14. Created using clipart © 2017 by Presenter Media and the Open Source Initiative. Used by permission.

Figure 8.15. Created using clipart © 2017 by Presenter Media and the Open Source Initiative. Used by permission.

Figure 8.16. Created using clipart © 2017 by Presenter Media and the Open Source Initiative. Used by permission.

Figure 8.17. Created using clipart © 2017 by Presenter Media and the Open Source Initiative. Used by permission.

Figure 8.18. Created using clipart © 2017 by Presenter Media and the Open Source Initiative. Used by permission.

Chapter 9

Figure 9.1. "Impact of Computers" by Emily Evans is a product of work by Chemeketa Press. All rights reserved.

Figure 9.2. "U+2117" by Estoy Aquí is licensed under CC0 Public Domain (https://commons.wikimedia.org/wiki/File:U%2B2117.svg).

Figure 9.3. "Copyright" by Masur is licensed under CC0 Public Domain (https://commons.wikimedia.org/wiki/File:Copyright.svg).

Figure 9.4. "Intellectual Property" by Faith Martinmaas is a product of work by Chemeketa Press. All rights reserved.

Figure 9.5. "Flag of Edward England" by WarX, edited by Manuel Strehl is licensed under CC BY-SA 3.0 (https://commons.wikimedia.org/wiki/File:Flag_of_Edward_England.svg).

Figure 9.6. "GAO logo" by GAO is licensed under Public Domain (www.gao.gov).

Figure 9.7. "MPAA logo" by MPAA is copyrighted content. Used by permission (www.mpaa.org).

Figure 9.8. "ACM logo" by ACM is used under Fair Use guidelines (https://www.acm.org/).

Figure 9.9. "BCS logo" by BCS is copyrighted content. Used by permission (www.bcs.org).

Figure 9.10. "LOPSA logo" by LOPSA is used under Fair Use guidelines (www.lopsa.org).

CPSIA information can be obtained
at www.ICGtesting.com
Printed in the USA
FSHW020302021218
53915FS